STROKES OF GENIUS

STROKES OF GENIUS

FEDERER v NADAL
RIVALS IN GREATNESS

L. Jon Wertheim

First published in Great Britain in 2009 by
JR Books, 10 Greenland Street, London NW1 0ND
www.jrbooks.com

ISBN 978-1-906779-39-9

1 3 5 7 9 10 8 5 4 2

Printed in MPG Books, Bodmin Cornwall

For Judith Wertheim
and Lilly Barr

Strokes of Genius

Introduction

IF ATHLETIC RIVALS aren't outright enemies, they are—by definition—adversaries. They fight each other and race each other and try to hit tennis balls past each other. In the most textured cases, they represent different styles and sensibilities and values and heritages. More often than not, there is at least a touch of dislike between them. All that competition, all that comparison, all that familiarity? Hell, yes, it can breed contempt.

But there's also a certain closeness. Bracketed together as they are, most rivals have the good sense to know that, finally, they are better for the existence of their nemesis. Sure, Nicklaus deprived Palmer of a bunch of trophies, just as Magic robbed Bird of a few more NBA titles. And vice versa. But they also pushed each other to greater heights. Sure, chess masters Boris Spassky and Bobby Fischer laid bare each other's imperfections and weaknesses that they would not have wanted to be exposed. But they also forced each other to improve and innovate. Sure, Frazier could have done without getting his face resculpted by Ali. But they also gave each other's achievements some context, some heft. In the end, rivals end up becoming intertwined: *Well, we know Ali was good because he beat Frazier, who was so good that he beat Ali.*

The peculiar dimensions of rivalry, the necessary distance and the necessary proximity, are laid bare in tennis. Positioned on opposite sides of the net, rivals spend hours engaged in wordless debate, swapping points and counterpoints and clever rejoinders, probing for weaknesses and setting traps. They're out there alone, cordoned off from outside influence. Unlike boxing, there are no cornermen plying them with Vaseline, encouragement, and instruction during breaks in the action. Unlike golf, the competition is simultaneous. A tennis player can't walk down the fairway while his rival takes his backswing. Truly, tennis is the most gladiatorial sport going.

At the same time, there's the built-in collegiality. Tennis rivals may face off a half-dozen times a year or more. They're forever running into each other in this Cincinnati hotel lobby or that Monte Carlo restaurant. They play on the same tour and often share the same management team and shoe sponsor. And sandwiched between all that on-court competition? Before the match, players spend ten minutes warming up together. (For kicks, try to analogize this to other sports: "Hey Joe, before we start to box in earnest, mind if I whap you a few times with my left hand?" "Sure, Muhammad.") And the instant the contest ends, tennis players head to the net for the ritual handshake.

This intimacy, forced as it may be, is particularly pronounced at Wimbledon. At the All England Lawn Tennis and Croquet Club, the top players—most of the highest seeds and former champions—share a locker room separate from the rank and file. It's not unlike one of those plush, fresh-smelling lounges at the airport, dividing the elite first-class fliers from the great unwashed in coach. Tastefully appointed with birch lockers and high-definition TVs on the walls, this enclave is not much bigger than your average living room. A player sneezes or belches and the others in the room know it. It's here that the top players gather when they're not on the court. High school wrestlers, junior college fencers, intramural soccer players, they wouldn't imagine sharing a locker room with their opponents. Yet at Wimbledon players get dressed alongside the same counterparts whom they'll engage in combat later in the afternoon.

So it was that at 13:00 Greenwich Mean Time on July 6, 2008, an hour or so before they were to face each other in the 122nd Wimbledon final—the most important match of the year's most important tournament—Switzerland's Roger Federer and Spain's Rafael Nadal came face to face. Federer was sitting in front of his usual locker, No. 66, relaxing on a pine bench, when Nadal trudged in and headed for locker 101 maybe a dozen paces away. Inasmuch as one man considered the other an interloper or a space invader—the groom spying the bride in advance of the wedding ceremony—they suppressed any outrage. Federer smiled wryly as if to say, "So, I guess we meet again." He looked genial and unthreatening. Nadal nodded in response, neither coldly nor warmly. Then each went back to pretending he had the room to himself.

Federer and Nadal form the most dynamic rivalry, not just in tennis but in all of contemporary sport. Together they have created a firewall, dividing themselves from the rest of the field. One or the other had won fourteen of the last sixteen Major Championships. For more than a century, no two men had played each other in both the French Open and the Wimbledon finals in the same year; Nadal and Federer had done it three years running. The 2008 Wimbledon final marked their eighteenth encounter. At the time, Nadal led the head-to-head face-offs eleven to six, including all three matches they'd played previously that year—though it should be noted that most of the matches were fought on his preferred surface of clay. Four Sundays earlier, Nadal had pasted Federer in the French Open final in Paris. The victory was so comprehensive (scoreline: 6–1, 6–3, 6–0) and so unworthy of their rivalry that it embarrassed both players. Nadal tried to avoid going into the locker room afterward, lest he glimpse Federer. Immediately after the match, Federer wore a brave face in public, but within days he would characterize the defeat as "brutal." Nadal's analysis was more charitable: "I played an almost perfect match and Roger made more mistakes than he usually does."

Yet Nadal was still consigned to No. 2 in the rankings, Federer having inhabited the top spot for 230 straight weeks and counting, a tennis record. What's more, Federer had beaten Nadal in the previous two Wimbledon finals—the 2007 edition was a five-set insta-classic. The loss had driven Nadal to tears and left him to wonder if he had squandered his best opportunity to win the one title he coveted most.

Beyond the records, their rivalry was heightened by clashing styles. One could spend hours playing the compare-and-contrast game. Federer versus Nadal embodies righty versus lefty. Classic technique versus ultramodern. Feline light versus taurine heavy. Middle European restraint and quiet meticulousness versus Iberian bravado and passion. Dignified power versus an unapologetic, whoomphing brutality. Zeus versus Hercules. Relentless genius versus unbending will. Polish versus grit. Metrosexuality versus hypermuscular hypermasculinity. A multitongued citizen of the world versus an unabashedly provincial homebody. A private-jet flier versus a steerage passenger. A Mercedes driver versus a Kia driver.

The tennis salon's comparison of Federer's evolved beauty with Nadal's Neanderthal drudge is as unfair as it is crass. You can accept the premise that they're both artists even though they're of decidedly different schools. Federer is a delicate, brush-stroking impressionist, and Nadal is a dogged, freewheeling abstract expressionist.

Although less than five years separate them—Federer's DOB 8/8/81, Nadal's DOB 6/6/86—they are on opposite sides of a generation gap. (Federer counts among his best friends a married Swiss investment banker in his late thirties; Nadal's *gran amigos* are mostly PlayStation savants in their early twenties.) Amazingly, they both have the exact same physical dimensions, 185 cm and 85 kg (6'1", 188 lbs.), but they could scarcely be more corporeally different. Federer is lithe and wiry, all sinewy strength and fast-twitch muscle. Nadal is built as if he could have had a career as an NFL halfback—if not a UFC cage fighter—had his tennis pursuit not panned out so magnificently.

Now, even in the locker room, awkwardly passing the time together/apart as rain delayed the start of their third straight Wimbledon final, their differences were glaringly apparent. Befitting a player preparing to compete in the final for the sixth straight year, undefeated at Wimbledon since 2002, Federer radiated calm. As one neutral observer later put it, "It was almost as if he were stoned." He sat on the bench smiling and cracking cocktail-party jokes. Having drained a twenty-ounce bottle of Pepsi that accompanied the plate of pasta primavera he ate for lunch, Federer munched one of his beloved Kit Kat chocolate bars. (At Federer's behest, the club had stocked them in the locker room, along with the bananas that other, lesser players had requested.) Severin Lüthi, the captain of the Swiss Davis Cup team and the closest thing Federer had to a coach that week, sat nearby. But when they spoke, it was mostly about matters other than tennis. Single-handedly setting back the field of sports psychology a good decade, Federer did no visualization or other mental exercises. He resembled a rock star lounging backstage before a gig he had performed innumerable times.

The previous night, at the house he was renting near the

courts, Nadal tossed in his bed. Images of his two previous Wimbledon finals invaded his thoughts—first a disappointing and then a devastating loss to Federer—and as much as he tried to banish them, they kept screaming back. He listened to music, got up to watch movies. He finally fell asleep at 4 A.M. and woke up at 9:30. When Nadal made it to the breakfast table, he saw that, for the first time all tournament, it was raining. "Finally, it's Wimbledon!" he joked.

Now, swinging his arms wildly and taking practice strokes in the locker room a few feet from Federer's head, Nadal cut the classic figure of a warrior preparing for battle. He had just taken a cold shower, and with his sympathetic nervous system kicking into high gear, Nadal was in fight-or-flight mode. His heart rate surely jackhammering, stress hormones coursing through his body, his pupils enlarged, he stretched and paced and pissed, making sure his urine was pale and odorless, an indication that his body was properly hydrated. Even when he tried to conserve energy, he fiddled with the tight bands of tape below his knees, worn to prevent the patellar tendinitis that has bothered him in the past. As if afflicted with low-grade OCD, he rifled through his swollen racket bag again and again. Another ritual, he lowered and raised his socks until they were precisely the same height. Sitting nearby, Nadal's uncle and coach, Toni Nadal, offered motivational bromides in intense staccato bursts: "There is no such word as 'cannot.'" "Do what you have to do." "Obligations are obligations."

At around 2:15 P.M., half an hour after their initial starting time, Federer and Nadal were advised that the sky, though still inky, had stopped spitting raindrops and the tarp tent protecting Centre Court was being deflated and disassembled. Federer and Nadal walked out of the locker room, wended down a long carpeted hallway, and slowly descended a set of stairs leading to the court. With Nadal walking ten feet ahead, they passed a photograph of Bjorn Borg and John McEnroe's Wimbledon final in 1980, the match against which all other tennis clashes are judged.

Here again, the Federer-Nadal differences were italicized and in boldface. Having outgrown the cream, gold-trimmed *Great Gatsby* blazer he'd worn without irony (and, miraculously, pulled off without mockery) in past years, Federer was now clad in a cream, gold-trimmed cardigan straight out of *Brideshead Revisited*—conservative attire that represented a sense of respect and history. The sweater, made by Nike, was sold in the Wimbledon gift shop for the larcenous price of £260, and only 230 had been produced, an inventory made to correspond with the 230 consecutive weeks Federer had spent ranked No. 1.

Nadal, who would sooner wear a grass skirt than a $500 cardigan sweater, donned a white warm-up. Federer wore classic tennis shorts cinched with a belt; Nadal wore his customary clamdiggers that sagged below the knees, no belt required. Federer's ration of hair was carefully styled, while Nadal's simply draped down his olive-skinned neck. They both wore Nike headbands and white Nike socks that poked out of white Nike shoes.

Just before walking on the court, they endured a prematch interview, an excruciating drill that requires players to offer a sound bite or two. The "host networks" negotiate this access as a condition of their hefty TV rights fee, and the players, without benefit of union protection, are forced to abide it. Still in their mental spaces, the players clearly resent this intrusion and offer a banquet of clichés. *It should be a good match. Winning the first set will be key. I need to serve well. I'm going to try my best and we'll see what happens.*

Yet even these hollow phrases can be pregnant with meaning. When Federer stood before the interviewer, he remarked,

"I feel good [but] it might be a tough day with the rain and everything and a tough opponent so it should be interesting," betraying what sports shrinks call "negative mental hygiene." When Nadal was asked a similar question about the rain delay and the inauspicious forecast, he rocked his head from side to side and shrugged, his default gesture. In his thick accent, he said softly, "The rain is for both [of us], so no problems. I just accept the weather conditions and I just play."

For all the small, quaint rituals that make professional tennis at once so thoroughly endearing and so thoroughly easy to mock—the church-like quiet of the crowd, the outmoded terminology, the players' insincere apologies after hitting winning shots off the frame of the racket—here's a personal favorite: the players carry their own rackets and bags onto the court. Tennis's top stars are among the most recognized athletes on the planet, wealthy to the point of abstraction, flush with entourages and Gulfstreams at the ready. But when they go to work, they lug their own crap, looking less like celebrities than itinerant backpackers in search of the Budapest youth hostel. The underlying symbolism is unmistakable: the minute your feet—shod as they may be in Nikes you're paid millions to endorse—hit the ground, you're on your own. In tennis, self-sufficiency is everything.

Yet in the final of Wimbledon, this rite is suspended. After six rounds of schlepping their own racket bags, the last two players in the Wimbledon draw are accorded concierge service. Though he admitted to feeling "empty and awkward," Federer surrendered his possessions to a court attendant and walked out unencumbered. Nadal did not. Tradition be damned, it was going to make him feel bereft, as if he were going into a duel without his .38. He gave up his bag but insisted on keeping one of his rackets in his left hand. No disrespect, he would later contend. He was a creature of habit and didn't want to be displaced from "my ritual, my very important ritual."

Word had spread throughout the complex that the rain delay was over and the match would begin. The capacity crowd of fifteen thousand parishioners filed into Centre Court of Wimbledon, a venue inevitably, but accurately, described as a "tennis cathedral." Most of the crowd wore its Sunday best: the women in Lilly Pulitzer dresses the color of jelly beans; the men with their Oxbridge good looks and Paul Smith shirts. (It was, by all appearances, a big year for vertical stripes.) But — more proof that Wimbledon has evolved from a garden party of the British landed gentry to an international sporting event — walking the concourse one also sees turbans and yarmulkes, and hears many tongues other than English. Inasmuch as crowd shots tend to look like pointillist paintings, Wimbledon's canvas is unmistakably multicolored.

John McEnroe settled into the small, glassed-in NBC broadcast booth — a terrarium directly behind the court, a few feet up from the grass surface — where he'd spend the rest of the afternoon and, as it would turn out, evening. Wearing a magnificent gray suit to match his magnificent gray mane of hair, Bjorn Borg sat in the front row of the Royal Box behind the baseline amid various dignitaries. Present, too, were other members of tennis's Mount Rushmore. Looking like a human trophy with his lacquered gold hair, Boris Becker represented both Eurosport network and German television, and Martina Navratilova worked for the American network Tennis Channel. Billie Jean King strolled regally on the grounds, as did Manuel Santana, the last Spanish male to win Wimbledon, in 1966. (This was decidedly another era: on the day of the final against Dennis Ralston, Santana rode to the All England Club on the London Underground.) Rumor had it — false, it turned out — that newlywed Chris Evert and her husband, the

Australian golfer Greg Norman, would stop by on their honeymoon. Say this about Mother Tennis: she takes care of her own. Old tennis soldiers don't fade away; they come back with special access credentials.

A veteran of the finals choreography, Federer went directly to the net for the ceremonial coin flip, where a child, often one with a chronic illness, is summoned to play a small role in the match, helping to determine which player serves first. In this case, Blair Manns, a thirteen-year-old Macaulay Culkin lookalike from Gloucester who suffers from a pulmonary disease, had the honors. He represented the British Lung Foundation. In addition to scoring an autographed poster of the finalists, he and his folks also received choice tickets for the match. Now Blair and Federer stood at the net. "Are you going to enjoy the match today?" Federer asked amiably. The kid nodded, too nervous to keep the conversation going.

The two were joined by Pascal Maria, the chair umpire for the match, and by the tournament referee, Andrew Jarrett. The quartet waited . . . and waited . . . and waited. Nadal sat in his chair, sipping Evian, chewing on an energy bar, folding his sweats, and indulging his longtime ritual of sipping from each of two bottles of water, one colder than the other, and then arranging the bottles just so, with the labels pointing toward the side of the court he'd occupy first. (And to think that Federer is usually cast as the anal one.) Impatience transparent on his face, Federer rocked back and forth and took practice swings near the net. Surely this affronted his Swiss sense of punctuality. The match had already been postponed by rain and the forecast was grim; why was Nadal taking his sweet time? Nadal seemed not to share the same sense of occasion, and clearly this was part of Federer's annoyance. According to a member of the Nadal entourage, in the players' box Federer's girlfriend,

Mirka Vavrinec, watched the Spaniard's dallying and muttered, "Oh, come on."

After a full minute of self-indulgence, Nadal trotted to the net. Having molted his warm-ups, he wore a sleeveless white tank top. It was made of a wicking microfiber that served the dual function of displacing his copious sweat and accentuating his propane-tank biceps. Perhaps flustered by the delay, young Blair Manns tossed the coin without asking either player to call it in midair. Jarrett intercepted the coin. Nervous smiles all around. Blair flipped it again. This time Federer correctly predicted heads, entitling him to serve first. But really it was beside the point. They had yet to strike the first ball, and already, intentionally or not, Nadal had struck a psychological blow.

Federer and Nadal then stood together for a ceremonial photograph and, like fighters touching gloves before a bout, tapped rackets. As Federer demurely walked away to begin the five-minute warm-up, Nadal turned and bolted from the net to the baseline in the manner of a giddy young bull. (N.B.: The Nadal–rampaging bull analogies and metaphors are inevitable, particularly since bull logos adorn even his Nike shoes. We'll try to limit the use of such imagery.) Running low to the ground, he performed a quick split step and then jogged along the baseline. Though Nadal dismisses this as another ritual, it functions as one more psychological salvo. Message: *Pack a lunch, hombre, because I'm going to be coming for you all day.*

Even in his warm-up, Federer is the picture of seamless efficiency. There's virtually no wasted movement. Like all great athletes, he has a natural mind-body connection. Whatever his brain imagines, his body executes. Clearly eager to start the match, Federer glanced several times at the courtside clock. He hit a few of his practice serves while standing inside the baseline. On the other end of the court, Nadal was all exertion. He thrust and pounded and unfurled his left-handed sidewinding strokes, punctuating his shots—his practice shots—with an onomatopoeic *fwwwwuuumph*. Already his white tank top was irrigated with sweat.

It was 14:35 GMT when the warm-up ended and Pascal Maria, the high priest in the umpire's chair, intoned, "Ready. Play."

And did they ever.

Centre Court

THERE WAS A NOTABLE absence at Wimbledon in 2008. Gone were the pigeons that used to nest in the Centre Court rafters and girders and then alight on the court, drawing spasms of laughter from the crowd, no matter how many times they had seen this spectacle before. All the nooks and crannies of the building made for deluxe accommodations; all that high-quality grass and seed on the court made for fine dining. Centre Court was a natural pigeon habitat, and the lead-colored birds had been as much a part of the tournament tableau as the Pimm's Cups and the all-white attire.

But the pigeons distracted the players, and as All England Club officials put it, in their delicate way, "Their detritus could be problematic." So the club enlisted Rufus, a Harris's hawk, natural predator of pigeons. Each morning, Rufus would soar menacingly above the grounds, and by the time the matches began, the pigeons would have vanished, been expelled from their homes. This bit of Darwinism was as good a metaphor as any for the tennis that would unfold on the courts. The theme of the tournament: the predator instincts of Rafael Nadal pitted against the territorial instincts of Roger Federer.

Asserting that Federer had won Wimbledon for five years running would, while true, have somehow understated the case. Federer *owned* Wimbledon during that time. No, check that. He *was* Wimbledon. As he accumulated trophies and tied Bjorn Borg's record of five consecutive titles, all the while fitting in so flawlessly, Federer came to overtake the event. The grass underfoot accentuated his fluid movements and his singular—which is to say, multiple—abilities: all that graceful volleying, those brilliantly angled flicks, those imaginative pieces of shotmaking. And Federer's conservative, decorous behavior played pitch-perfectly at an event dripping with tradition. This wasn't one of those ornery sluggers with a baseball cap turned backward, a display of tattoos and jewelry, mispronouncing the tournament "Wim-bull-TIN." He was a kid the adults at Wimbledon—Wim-bull-DUN—could love. Here was a classicist nostalgic for an era that predated him. Here was a European stylist who embraced all the quirks and customs and formalities of the tournament. When he won, he was so filled with reverence and appreciation (and adrenaline) that he would cry when receiving the trophy. This transparent emotion endeared Federer to the fans even more than the preceding Wimbledon monarch, Pete Sampras, who while comparably successful was stiff and exacting, not brilliant and elegantly charismatic the way Federer is perceived to be.

If Wimbledon came to represent a veritable Federer jubilee, he was just as successful and popular at the other stops on the tennis caravan. Federer became the top-ranked player in the Association of Tennis Professionals (ATP) in 2004, ushering in the Federer Era, the most dominant regime in tennis history. In four years he won eleven of the sixteen Majors—or, to use the bastardized term, Slams—the sport's four bedrock events. He won on all continents, on all surfaces, against all opponents. Entire forests would have to be felled to reprint the gaudy statistics supporting the dominance of the Federer Era. To limit this exercise to one such example: from 2004 to 2007, his match record was 315–24.

More remarkable still, Federer won not with unanswerable, might-makes-right power, but with flourish and flair. His game relies on precision and nuance and opulent talent. For all the modern touches, his style is mostly a throwback, what with his one-handed backhand, his simple handshake grip, his fondness for net play. It is a rare sports marriage of style and substance. The descriptions of Federer's game are often pulled from art and light: it's poetry, ballet, a renaissance painting, a symphony. He's an artist, a calligrapher, a maestro, a virtuoso on a stringed instrument. He's luminescent, phosphorescent, incandescent. The lowbrow observer who termed Federer's style as viscerally enjoyable "tennis porn," well, he was onto something too.

Major titles are the measuring stick for tennis excellence, and Federer began 2008 with an even dozen for his career, putting him two away from the all-time record that poor Sampras had established a few years back and, it appeared, would be afforded precious little time to savor. Federer had never won the French Open—the one entry missing from his CV—but unlike Sampras, he was hardly allergic to clay. Put all the factors in the cement mixer and, in the eyes of many, myself included, Federer was at least on the precipice of taking the mythical title of tennis's Greatest of All Time, the GOAT, in message board shorthand.

Yet in 2008, the Federer Empire was, if not crumbling, showing some troubling signs of decay. A bout with mononucleosis had cost Federer twenty days of practice during tennis's winter off-season (inasmuch as you can call a six-week winter break an off-season). In his first tournament of 2008, Federer lost in the semifinals of the Australian Open to Novak Djokovic, a self-enchanted, bristle-haired Serb who, unlike many of his peers, is thoroughly unawed by Federer. After the match, Djokovic's mother, Dijana, crowed to reporters, "The king is

dead. Long live the king." This bold pronouncement of regi-
cide was (a) absurd, (b) tactless in the extreme, and (c) strikingly at odds with Federer's grace. But as the 2008 season unfolded, more and more observers came to share, if not to fully
articulate, her thoughts.

Still a step slow, Federer slogged through the next few
months. In March, he played an exhibition against Sampras
in New York's venerable, dilapidated Madison Square Garden,
a match, Federer confided to a friend, that was "a million-
dollar stopover" between tournaments in Dubai (where Federer
has a residence) and Palm Springs. The evening was great fun,
a much-needed boost for a sport with a diminishing profile
in the United States. New York's tennis scene turned out in
force, as did Donald Trump, Tiger Woods, Luke Wilson, and
the rest of the canapé-eating celebrity set, to watch the two
hegemonic male players of the Open Era, when amateurs and
professionals played together. There was, however, this minor
inconvenience: Federer required a third-set tiebreaker to sub-
due Sampras, then a thirty-six-year-old full-time father who
hadn't played a sanctioned tennis match since 2002. Though
the match's outcome didn't appear to be fixed—as is sometimes the case with "exos"—neither did it appear that Federer
was playing anywhere close to his customary level.

In the spring, Federer developed a hideous pimple on the
right side of his face. In a mustache-on-the-*Mona-Lisa* kind
of way, it was jarring to see a scrupulous and handsome athlete wearing the type of unseemly turbo-zit that ruins junior
prom night. (A real "Yahoo! Answers" discussion topic: Does
anybody know what that is on R. Federer's face?) The blem-
ish was symbolic of Federer's season. His spring was pocked
by losses to mortals (Mardy Fish? Radek Stepanek?), to creditable opponents (the Andys, Roddick and Murray), and to his
nemesis (Nadal). Apart from the losses, there were other indi-

cations that Federer had misplaced his muse. Usually a model of poise and sportsmanship, he was so overcome with frustration in a tournament in Hamburg, Germany, that he smacked a ball out of the stadium. Playing against Djokovic in Monte Carlo, Federer became enraged by the vocal midmatch chattering of Djokovic's omnipresent parents, who were seated behind the baseline. After they objected vocally to a line call, Federer turned to them and snapped disdainfully, "Be quiet! Okay?" Of course, any other mega-athlete in a similar position of power would have yelled something more emphatic and profane. But still, it was out of character. For Federer, this was the equivalent of "Fuck you."

On sheer talent, Federer carved his way through the draw of the 2008 French Open. He was to face Nadal, the three-time champion, in the final. It was beautifully scripted. If Federer could summon his best tennis and defeat Nadal—invading his rival's kingdom, as it were—it would mark perhaps the most significant title of his career. He'd complete the so-called Career Slam—winning all four Major titles—and in doing so cement his legacy as the Greatest of All Time. Case closed, discussion over. This was precisely the kind of scenario that the Great Ones relish.

If Federer laid an egg in the final, it was of the ostrich variety. The same rational thinking and self-awareness that make him such a likable champion can serve him poorly on the court. Midway through the match, he became convinced it wasn't his day. And he could not or would not try to trick himself into thinking otherwise. Federer shook his head, furrowed his considerable eyebrows, and scowled as he lumbered to his chair on changeovers. Once he gave himself no chance to win, he figured he'd do the next best thing and get the hell offstage as soon as possible. Operating at an auctioneer's pace, he made only halfhearted efforts to retrieve balls. The third set flew by in twenty-seven minutes, a soufflé-like collapse that ended 6–0. It was strictly a cover-your-eyes affair.

To his credit, Nadal gave Federer no chance to reconsider his thinking. Almost merciless in his accuracy, Nadal went entire games striking the ball perfectly. Nadal claimed that he barely noticed Federer's vacant effort. Not so the rest of his entourage. Before the match had ended, Toni Nadal, Rafael's numinous coach and uncle, nudged his neighbors in the stands and used the word "bizarre" to describe Federer's disposition. "I must read the papers tomorrow to find out what was going on in his head," Toni said after the match. "I never sensed any determination. He never put himself in that state. I was watching his face. Closed. He wasn't sending any messages to Rafa. He didn't have a winner's mentality. It wasn't the real Roger."

At some level, Federer had fallen victim to his own dizzyingly high standards. By any objective measure, he was having a very respectable year. But, be it on account of the mono, his advancing age (almost a doddering twenty-seven!), or simply the finite shelf life of excellence, it was all so . . . un-Federerian. When you win ninety-two percent of your matches and then suddenly reach the halfway point of a season with only one title (a rinky-dink one at that, the Estoril Open) to your credit, the contrast is conspicuous. In Federer's own words, he had created "a monster" with his unsurpassed success and the expectations it wrought.

Even the more sober analysts, not quite prepared to issue a coroner's report on Federer's career just yet, conceded that the 2008 Wimbledon was freighted with significance. If he won for the sixth straight time, well, all was right with the world. If he lost, maybe it was time to table that GOAT talk for a while. And if he lost to Nadal, for all intents relinquishing the No. 1 ranking in the process, it was this simple: after a glorious four-year term, there would be a new administration in men's tennis.

Federer's grass court campaign began auspiciously enough. The week after his French Open debacle, he won the Wimbledon tune-up event in Halle, Germany, running his winning streak on sod to fifty-nine matches. But when he arrived in the village of Wimbledon and settled into his rental house a few miles from the All England Club—a mansion owned, coincidentally, by a family with the surname Borg, no relation—the dirges began anew. "Is Fed Dead?" asked one London tabloid. Djokovic, the brash *arriviste* who had been lacking from the ATP's cast, declared that Federer was "vulnerable." Boris Becker, the three-time Wimbledon champion, tipped Nadal to win and gave Federer "only a small chance." Bjorn Borg—whose record of five straight Wimbledon titles Federer was attempting to surpass—picked not only Nadal but Djokovic ahead of Federer. Borg also asserted that, no, it would not surprise him if Federer were to lose the title and disappear from tennis altogether.

Federer traversed the high road. During his conclaves with the media, he shrugged off intimations of his mortality. "I haven't been reading and I haven't been listening to what's been said about me," he lied. Asked specifically about Borg's uncharitable remarks, Federer winced. "I mean, look, it's his opinion. I don't mind what he says. Obviously at the moment he has a microphone under his face and people ask him many, many things. Once he'll sound more critical, once he'll sound more positive." Did he ever consider confronting Borg? "Oh, no," he said a few months later, "I would never approach him with something like that. I don't want a problem with the King."

But this Wimbledon deathwatch, tinged as it was with so much *schadenfreude,* infuriated Federer. He wins everything in sight for four years, makes all the right moves, and brings all sorts of dignity and honor to the sport. Then this? *A couple of substandard months and all these slings and arrows? Is there no accrued goodwill?* "To be honest, I was surprised by how extreme it was. I was hearing, 'He's not going to win a thing anymore.' You try to ignore it, not let it bother you, but . . ."

He was in an unwinnable position. If he defended himself from the critics, downplayed his slump, and pronounced himself, as he did, "the big favorite obviously for Wimbledon," he risked coming off sounding arrogant or, worse yet, delusional. If he fought back and pointed out the hypocrisy — Borg? predicting someone else would walk away from the sport after a loss? — he'd be diminishing himself. Tellingly, it was Federer's colleagues who took up his defense and offered voices of reason. Asked if he agreed with the premise that Federer was vulnerable, Nadal rolled his eyes. "Yes, a lot. He didn't lose a set [last week]. And he's won fifty-nine matches without a loss. Come on!"

Surrounded by a swelling entourage, Federer spent his downtime at the rental manor. He visited the London Zoo and went shopping and dined at a few trendy restaurants. But unlike past years, he spent as little time as possible at the All England Club. Early in the tournament, as Federer tried to make a hasty getaway from the players' patio, a pair of hangers-on cornered him and asked him to pose for a photo. "I wish there were two of me," he muttered. Federer being Federer, he dropped his bag, draped his arms over the man and his wife, mustered something approximating a smile, and waited for the flash.

Then there was Nadal. After winning his fourth straight French Open title, he didn't linger in Paris. It was as if once the coating of clay had been washed off his body in the locker room shower, the memories went with it. He and his camp shared a subdued celebratory dinner that Sunday night, then it was on to grass. Nadal's long-avowed ambition, despite his clay court provenance (and success), had always been to win on the lawns of Wimbledon. He'd come close in 2007. Now, playing the best tennis of his life and with Federer appearing a bit, well, vulnerable, Nadal figured, "Maybe it's my time." Though it was superfluous, he had an added motivation: if he could win, he'd be virtually assured of ascending from the No. 2 position he'd held for a record three straight years. No longer would he be the middle manager trapped under Federer's glass ceiling.

When Nadal defended his French Open title in 2006, he was scheduled to play the Queen's Club event in London, a grass court tune-up that begins the day after the Roland Garros final. Worried that Nadal might be so exhausted that he'd lavish himself with a week off, the Queen's Club tournament director offered to charter a helicopter to shuttle Nadal from Paris to London. Cool, thought Nadal, who'd never considered pulling out of Queen's anyway. Not cool, thought his uncle Toni. They had already booked their tickets on the Eurostar, the high-speed train that runs from Paris to London under the English Channel. "We're not wasting that money," Toni said flatly. They declined the private helicopter and took the train.

For Nadal and his camp, the Eurostar ride from Paris to London had hardened into ritual. So the day after winning his fourth French Open, Nadal trudged through the Gare du Nord alongside the other commuters and businessmen. He posed for a few photos and signed some autographs, but otherwise he was just another independent contractor heading off on a Monday morning to do some business in London. After two hours aboard the train spent napping and playing cards, Nadal arrived at King's Cross St. Pancras station, having overcome his fear of traveling underwater.

By early afternoon, less than twenty-four hours after winning the most esteemed clay court title, Nadal clocked a two-hour practice on grass, altering his footwork, hitting his returns of serve earlier, flattening out his strokes, slicing his backhand, guiding the ball to stay low to the ground. Nadal's making such material adjustments to his game was another indication that his stated goal of winning Wimbledon was no talking point, no bit of agent-inspired misdirection. The next day, heralding this quick transition to grass, a breathless tabloid headline read: "Nadal: You Won't Like Me When I Turn Green."

The Queen's Club courts, players say, are even faster than Wimbledon's lawns, which made Nadal's seamless transition all the more impressive. In the course of five days at Queen's Club, he beat five opponents, including some of the most accomplished grass court practitioners. Against Ivo Karlovic, a six-foot-ten Croatian whose serves appear to travel as far on the vertical axis as they do on the horizontal, Nadal played better in the tiebreakers and won 6–7, 7–6, 7–6. Against Roddick, the thunderbolt-serving American, Nadal played opportunistically and won in straight sets. Betraying emotion that hadn't been offered into evidence earlier in the week, Nadal, clearly motivated, beat Djokovic in the final. It marked the twenty-eighth title of Nadal's career and his second in seven days. And he became the first Spaniard to win a grass court event in thirty-six years. It had been an ideal week. He got in his grass court prep work. He sustained his swollen confidence. He put the rest of the field on alert. An afterthought, perhaps, but he also pocketed nearly $150,000 for the week. And then he left England to fly home to Majorca for a few days, to fish for tuna in the Mediterranean with his dad.

In keeping with the tradition whereby the defending champion plays the first match on Centre Court, Federer christened Wimbledon 2008 at 1 P.M. on the first Monday afternoon. The court, the closest thing tennis has to the Elysian Fields, had a new look this year: a pair of seventy-ton trusses and a space-shuttle-looking fixture protruding from the top of the complex, part of Centre Court's retractable, translucent roof, scheduled for completion in 2009.

Federer sported a different look too. He debuted that cardigan as he walked onto the lawn with his racket bag slung over one shoulder and what can only be described as a white leather man-purse slung over the other.

The draw had disgorged Dominik Hrbaty, a veteran Slovak, as a first opponent, and this was precisely Federer's kind of matchup. Unlike most dominant athletes — see Woods, Tiger — who choose to operate at an imposing remove from the rest of the field, Federer is an enlightened monarch, a benevolent despot on the friendliest terms with his colleagues/subjects. Hrbaty was a longtime friend, occasional doubles partner, and unapologetic Federer-phile. Though he had beaten Federer in the past, Hrbaty took the court with no genuine expectation of winning.

Under ideal conditions, congenially warm with no wind or humidity, it took Federer less than an hour to win the first two sets. Trailing in the third set 5–2, Hrbaty walked past his chair and sat next to him. "I looked over and there he was," Federer said. "He asked if he could sit next to me. I said sure, there's no problem, and there's an empty seat." The two men, notionally opponents, spent the ninety-second changeover chatting in the sun, a scene that could easily have epitomized the Federer

Era. Friendship, camaraderie, and warmth had bleached out the competition. When the umpire called time, Federer rose, served out the match, carefully gathered his gear, and that was that. As days at the office go, this one could scarcely have been easier.

The following day, Nadal made his 2008 Wimbledon debut against Andreas Beck, a twenty-two-year-old German who'd successfully snaked his way through the qualifying draw only to have the misfortune of encountering the sport's hottest player in his initial main draw match. Beck is prodigiously skilled at tennis, among the top 125 or so players on the planet, putting him in the top .00000002 percentile. Unfortunately, Nadal is another few decimal places over. An hour or so after losing to Nadal, in straight sets but with honor, Beck was still trying to process his opponent's level of play. "It's just not a game, what he's playing," Beck said, shaking his head. "It's unbelievable. I was thinking all the time, what the hell is he doing?" Did Beck at least feel he had *some* hope while he was holding his serve in the first set? "No. I had all the time no chance against him."

There's a cautionary Wimbledon saying: "You can't win the tournament in the first week. You can only lose it." But neither Federer nor Nadal looked to be in danger of losing. Federer returned to Centre Court the following day for his second match. His box, his section of reserved seats just off the far baseline, was peopled by an eclectic mix of characters: his agent (Tony Godsick), his mother (Lynette Federer), and his longtime girlfriend (Mirka Vavrinec) sat alongside Anna Wintour, the profoundly pregnant pop star Gwen Stefani, and Stefani's husband, Gavin Rossdale, once the front man for the band Bush. In both configuration and makeup, this section resembled an odd *Hollywood Squares* board. *Good answer, Gavin, but I'm going to take Gilbert Gottfried for the block!*

Stefani and Rossdale, a tennis junkie, had become friendly ·with Federer and Mirka, and they were regulars at big matches. When Federer spent time in southern California in 2007 before the Indian Wells tournament, he stayed at Stefani and Rossdale's home. During that visit, Federer practiced with Pete Sampras in Los Angeles, which, apart from making for an easy story for the tennis press, solidified their friendship. For their first session, they practiced on the court of the Stefani-Rossdale estate. Sampras wasn't comfortable with the assortment of tennis voyeurs fringing the court. He was surprised when Federer, nice guy that he was, indulged Rossdale in a hitting session later that afternoon. Sampras requested that the second practice session take place on the backyard court of his house in Beverly Hills. "It'll be more private," Sampras explained. Federer arrived at the appointed time, accompanied by Rossdale, who stayed and watched the two best players of the Open Era bat balls. "We took the gloves off that day," says Sampras.

Wintour, of course, is the editor of *Vogue,* the eccentric fashionista forever associated with the ruthless boss depicted in the book and movie *The Devil Wears Prada.* She'd met Federer in New York several years before and had become a good friend and borderline obsessive fan of his. Federer has surely appeared in *Vogue* more times than any other athlete. Wintour has been known to send suits to Federer's hotel rooms, simply because she's seen them and thought they'd look good on him. Though there are no sexual echoes, they've dined together at New York restaurants and she's turned up for his matches all over the globe. When Federer played Sampras in the Manhattan exhibition in March, *Vogue* was a sponsor and Wintour, in her trademark pageboy haircut and wearing oversized sunglasses indoors, sat in the front row.

The Wimbledon "backstage" area, the ominous-sounding Millennium Building, resembles a cruise ship with multiple decks—the interview room and press room on the bottom, a sunny patio above that, and an outdoor dining room on top. Before Federer's second match, Wintour was spotted on the patio level and asked by a reporter if she wouldn't mind answering a few quick questions about Federer. "On or off the record?" she replied warily. *Um, on, preferably.* "If you're going to ask me about Roger," she said, pausing dramatically, "Roger is brilliant." With that she turned and shuffled off. Some athletes attract young groupies of dubious virtue. Federer attracts fiftysomething magazine editors who send him fashionable sport coats.

Federer next faced Robin Soderling, a powerful but erratic Swede whose spiky hair and narrow, deeply set eyes give him the look of an angry drummer in a Scandinavian heavy-metal band. At Wimbledon in 2007, Soderling pushed Nadal to five sets, all the while poking fun at the Spaniard's rituals and leisurely pace. Nadal appeared genuinely wounded by this display, insinuating that Soderling was a bad person destined for hell. Asked about the Swede's mocking gestures, Nadal responded, "We will see what's happening in the end of the life, no?"

But if Soderling had been impertinent toward Nadal, he was thoroughly deferential toward Federer. Despite his fearsome, if irregular, bursts of power, Soderling was not in the same position as Federer on the food chain. And by the second set it was not a question of whether he would be defeated, but when and how. At one point, a journalist in the press section turned to Simon Barnes, a columnist for the London *Times*—for my deflated U.S. currency, as fine a sportswriter as there is today. Do you think, Barnes was asked, Federer ever got bored of playing tennis? Barnes responded: "Did van Gogh get bored when he painted at Arles?"

The draw gods continued to smile on Federer. For his

third match he played Marc Gicquel, a French veteran. When Federer made it from the seeded players' locker room to the lip of the court, Gicquel was already waiting. "*Ça va?*" Federer asked cheerily. French is one of four languages he speaks fluently. Sure, they were about to do battle on the court for a few hours, but to Federer it seemed only natural to pass a colleague and ask, "What's going on?"

Gicquel had neither the time nor the inclination to give a detailed answer. But it was going great for him. This third-round match represented the high-water mark of his career. A journeyman on the wrong side of thirty, Gicquel had never won a pro title—and likely never would—and recognized that playing a champion on Centre Court at Wimbledon was as good as it gets. The previous night, his wife had left their eighteen-month-old child at home in Paris and taken the Eurostar to London to be on hand.

Gicquel had been a late bloomer. He went to university and only launched his pro career at twenty-four, the age at which other players begin to contemplate retirement. He spent five years pinballing around the challenger circuit, the tennis equivalent of the minor leagues. The challengers express one of the great tragedies of sports. Fans see only the glory and riches accorded the stars. Federer, for instance, had recently crossed the $40 million mark in career prize money and earns much, much more in endorsements, bonuses, and appearance fees. As for Nadal, between his endorsements (Nike most notably) and prize money, he earns in excess of $20 million annually.

Underneath—and not far underneath—there dwells a sprawling underclass, lucky to live paycheck to paycheck, consigned to the "minors" or the "bush leagues," either term brutally uncharitable. These players dumpster-dive for ranking points that might afford them entry into the prequalifying draws of an ATP event, which might enable them to enter qualifying draws, which might enable them to enter main draws.

In tennis, players outside the top 150 in the rankings "grind it" in challenger events, held everywhere from European hamlets to Paraguayan villages to American backwaters. The prize money is negligible and players economize by billeting with local families (or sleeping three to a room at the local low-budget hostelry), stringing their own rackets, and often swiping dinner from the tournament buffet. (Fruit, good. Soup, bad.) The irony, of course, is that one could hardly conceive of worse working conditions for ambitious athletes.

Gicquel "ground it" mostly in Europe, though as recently as 2006 he traveled as far as Kyoto for an event, where he lost in the first round for a payday of $260. A compactly built, clean-cut baseliner, Gicquel has a pedestrian game that lacks both a glaring weakness and an obvious strength. Over the years, he made improvements where he could, upgrading his conditioning and consistency. Slowly he progressed, and by 2006 he'd escaped challenger purgatory, cracking the top 150, the threshold for making it financially. He bought an apartment in Paris near the Roland Garros complex, paid off various debts, and became a father. "Finally," he says, "you feel like a real pro tennis player."

Gicquel may have come to Wimbledon ranked a mere eighth among the French contingent, the Gauls able to mint top players in a way most other countries cannot. Yet he was hitting the ball soundly and was on the verge of piercing the top 50. In his first match, good fortune delivered: he advanced when his opponent, Kei Nishikori, a promising Japanese teenager, was forced to quit on account of a strained abdominal muscle. Gicquel then staved off a match point and survived a Serbian qualifier in five sets. Such is the randomness of the early rounds for tennis's rank and file: a few lucky breaks and a few shots separating a third-round advancement from a first-round defeat. While his thirty-one-year-old legs felt as if they had been filled with lead, Gicquel savored the thrill of playing Federer. He offered little resistance, but enjoyed the afternoon immensely. He winked at his wife as he left the court and pocketed $55,000 for the week.

As for Federer, the day after he won his match over Gicquel, 6–3, 6–3, 6–1, in eighty-one minutes, the *Daily Mail*'s headline read: "Fed Express Hits the Buffers." The *Sunday Express* somehow drew a similar conclusion from the match: "Roger Is Not Mr. Invincible." Meanwhile, Pat Cash, an ageless Australian who looks no different from when he won the men's singles title in 1987, predicted that Federer — the quintuple champion, mind you — was ripe for defeat. Little wonder, Federer couldn't escape Tennis Nation fast enough, and he retreated to his rental house, a sensory deprivation chamber where he didn't have to hear about his inevitable demise.

If Federer was a cipher at Wimbledon, Nadal was everywhere. He lingered at the All England Club after his matches. He pushed a shopping cart at the Tesco grocery store in Wimbledon village. At restaurants he dined al fresco, taking in the street scene. Nadal's rental place, much more modest than Federer's, was on Newstead Way, maybe a hundred yards from the club, and he didn't exactly conceal his residence. If the Spanish flag that sometimes hung from the shingles didn't provide enough of a clue, the yelling from inside — especially when Spain was playing in the Euro 2008 soccer tournament — was a dead giveaway. Nadal watched *Rocky* and *Terminator* on DVD as well as a video of the best goals in soccer history. He sacrificed hours at the altar of PlayStation. He read *The Boy in the Striped Pajamas,* a novel about the young son of a Nazi commandant. A friend of Nadal's called the compound "Camp Rafa." As in past years, Nadal invited journalists to stop by the house. It's no wonder that, though Federer is more popular among adults, the kids thrill to Nadal.

On most days, Nadal simply grabbed his bag and walked to the courts. More than a few ticket holders were surprised to walk down Somerset Road and see the tournament's second seed strolling alongside them. And those who missed seeing Nadal in person could still follow his daily doings. In exchange for a small donation to Nadal's philanthropic foundation, the London *Times* printed the player's daily blog. A sample post: "I went out to Wimbledon to do some grocery (?). Is that the word for shopping food? I guess so. I cooked . . . pasta with mushrooms, gambas, some onion at the beginning and these crab sticks. Not bad, believe me. Anyway I am going to bed now and finish the *Godfather.*"

Another quaint Wimbledon tradition: there is no play on the middle Sunday. The other Grand Slams hope to mimic the Olympics and stretch play over three weekends in order to maximize television revenue and gain additional ticket-selling sessions. To its great financial detriment, Wimbledon takes the opposite approach. Citing history and "a respect for our neighbors," the All England Club mandates that no matches be scheduled on the middle Sunday. The black iron gates are locked to the public. The courts are swaddled with tarps. The loudest sound on the grounds is the pealing of bells from St. Mary's Church up the road. The absence of play on Sunday can be problematic when rain constipates the match schedule. "You waste a whole day with no matches and you ask for trouble," Nadal complained, not unreasonably, the previous year, when inclement weather forced him to play on six consecutive days. But it's a welcome intermission. And it's reassuring to know that in at least one sector of the Sports Industrial Complex, tradition can still trump commerce.

At two o'clock on the afternoon of the middle Sunday, under a dome of clouds, Federer arrived on-site. Even on the off day, he complied with the "whites only" policy, wearing his Sunday best: the cardigan, white sweatpants, and a silver Rolex that he's paid to endorse. He'd booked a session at the Aorangi Terrace practice court behind Court 1 with Yves Allegro, an old friend. A Swiss doubles specialist who was approaching thirty—and whose ranking was approaching far greater heights—Allegro was no longer in the tournament, but he was on hand acting as the equivalent of a confidant in the Federer administration.

This is common in sports. Top players, wary of forming close friendships with potential opponents, seek out alliances with lesser lights, who are able to hang with them on the practice court and serve as dinner partners without posing a threat. Michael Jordan's best friend was not a fellow all-star but a journeyman, Rod Higgins. Andre Agassi befriended a little-known Armenian player, Sargis Sargsian. Nadal often keeps the company of a Spanish player, Bartolome Salva-Vidal, whose career-high ranking peaked at No. 693. Federer has Allegro. In return for loyalty and friendship, the star is often exceedingly generous. Higgins is the general manager of the Charlotte Bobcats, the NBA franchise of which Jordan is part owner. Agassi was known to enter events only on the condition that Sargsian was provided with a wild card. In the case of Allegro, Federer sometimes enters doubles events with him, putting money in the guy's pocket and giving him some exposure. He lets Allegro share in the trappings of celebrity, inviting him aboard his private plane, a mode of transport unknown to players with a career-high doubles ranking topping out at No. 32. And there's this story: Allegro's father runs a tennis club in Grone, Switzerland, a quiet town in the Alpine foothills. Several years ago, the club fell on hard times. Federer made a deal: pick a date and I'll show up to play an exhibition against Yves. Thousands of fans attended, and the club was back on a solid financial footing.

With Severin Lüthi, the Swiss Davis Cup captain, pinned against the back fence looking on, Federer and Allegro batted the ball back and forth on Practice Court 5. Because they used different rackets with different string tensions, each made a distinct sound, and the *thwick-thwock* resembled a metronome counting off musical beats. Watching Federer practice casually and lightly, one wouldn't guess that he was gunning for his sixth straight Wimbledon. But even fooling around—catching balls in midair on his strings, batting a forehand with the butt of his racket, hitting kick serves that landed in the corner of the service box, took a hard left, and bounded into the side fence—he offered a glimpse of his prodigious talent.

After an hour, his T-shirt saturated with sweat, Federer called it quits. He slapped five with Allegro and they both sat on their bags and chatted. As Federer rose to leave, he was approached by a player on the adjacent court, a lanky, mop-headed Brazilian, Andre Sa. Now thirty-one, Sa had been on the pro circuit since 1996. No slouch of a player, he had once reached the Wimbledon quarterfinals. Sheepishly, he asked if Federer would mind posing for a photo with him. Sa wanted a souvenir of the greatest player ever and didn't know how many more chances he'd get.

According to the tournament schedule, Nadal was slated to practice later in the afternoon. But at the appointed time, the court reserved for Nadal was vacant. Nadal, a club official explained to an annoying reporter, had come to the courts hours earlier with his agent, Carlos Costa. An avian-looking Spaniard, Costa was a former player once ranked as high as No. 10—though, typical for an Iberian player of his generation, Costa had never been beyond the second round of Wimbledon—and was a capable sparring partner for Nadal. The club official explained, "If you came to watch him, you didn't miss much tennis. Lots of laughing. And they kicked the tennis ball, football style. Then they left, I suppose to get ready to watch Spain in Euro 2008."

When the tournament began, Federer and Nadal were positioned on opposite poles of the draw, and like two magnets, they seemed destined to converge. By the fourth round, after 112 of the 128 competitors had been winnowed out, their showdown was almost a foregone conclusion. The most feared foe in Federer's half of the draw, Novak Djokovic, looked "vulnerable," to borrow a phrase, and was ousted by Marat Safin in the second round. In Nadal's half, his stiffest potential foe, Andy Roddick, was knocked out in the second round too.

Federer played his fourth-round match against Lleyton Hewitt, the last man to win Wimbledon before Federer. Hewitt's game was neither artistic (Federer) nor powerful (Roddick) nor violent (Nadal), but it hardly mattered. He was a fine athlete with quick feet, exquisite counterpunching skills, and above all, abundant heart/guts/spleen/backbone/balls—pick your anatomical metaphor.

If Federer prefers calm waters—fearful of dissonance and eager to befriend all—Hewitt's MO is the opposite. To him, conflict is fuel, competition is battle. With his parents egging him on, Hewitt has picked fights with the press, the ATP tour staff, other players, officials, Tennis Australia, gravity, Earth, the other planets. Whatever. Hewitt was engaged to Kim Clijsters, a terminally congenial Belgian who was once the top-ranked player in the Women's Tennis Association. But then the wedding was hastily called off. He burned through agents, managers, and coaches, seldom breaking up on amicable terms.

Eventually Hewitt exhausted his reserves of anger, and when he ran out of fights to pick (and lost a step of quickness because of a hip injury), his game went into steep decline. Now he played gamely against Federer, but at times he appeared to be less an opponent than a partner in the performance. Federer won 7–6, 6–2, 6–4, failing to drop a set yet again. As they approached the net to shake hands, Hewitt removed his baseball cap, a show of reverence for Federer.

Federer was asked whether he'd had any empathy for Hewitt during the match, this former top player and Wimbledon champ clearly at the caboose end of his career, a shard of his former self. "I mean, I feel bad for him that, you know, he's injured. That's where I feel bad for him for a split second. But at the same time he was still dangerous . . . I mean, I just feel bad, you know, that he has so many injury problems, that it's just not really working out for him. But by beating him, not in any way, no."

Nadal arrived for round four in a giddy state. The previous night, he'd put on a red jersey and watched the Spanish soccer team defeat Germany and win the European championships for the first time in forty-four years. He knew that it was around the same time that the last Spaniard, Manuel Santana, had won Wimbledon, and maybe fate had . . . never mind. Whenever that thought entered Nadal's head, he tried to banish it. When Spain won the soccer game, Nadal, deeply patriotic, celebrated like a kid, and Toni grew fearful that his nephew might be distracted. Instead, it had a galvanizing effect, and Nadal beat his next opponent, Mikhail Youzhny of Russia, handily.

To the fans watching Nadal position himself smack atop the baseline and zing his lefty lasers, it seemed inconceivable that he could be beaten. At least until Federer took the court.

Then, as the crowd watched the Swiss stylist serve brilliantly and play such authoritative tennis, it seemed inconceivable that *he* could be beaten. Until Nadal next played.

In the quarterfinals, Federer met Mario Ancic, a Croatian with the wingspan of a Cessna and the last man to have beaten Federer at Wimbledon, way back in 2002. As the hip-hop impresario Jay-Z—hilariously referred to as "Jay-Zed" by a BBC commentator—watched from behind the far baseline, Federer was scarcely tested, winning in straight sets. With the victory, he had reached his seventeenth straight Grand Slam semifinal. (Consider: Tiger Woods's equivalent streak of consecutive top-four finishes at major golf championships? Four.) As Federer put the finishing touches on another masterpiece, a fan yelled, "Get on with it. Bring on Andy." Unable to pretend he hadn't heard, Federer bit his lip trying to suppress a smile.

"Andy" was Andy Murray, the Scot saddled with the expectation of being the Great British Hope. In his previous match, Murray had rallied from two sets down to beat Richard Gasquet, a Frenchman as long on talent as he is short on mettle. It was great theater, watched by more than ten million Brits, and it inspired an intense, if short-lived, moment of irrational exuberance. Andy-monium, as someone called it.

Inasmuch as the Nadal-Murray quarterfinal had the feel of a Major Sporting Event, Nadal quickly drained any drama from the match. Had this been boxing, the referee would have called an early stoppage. As it was, they played until the end, Nadal thrashing Murray, the No. 12 player in the world at the time, on his home court in straight sets, surrendering just ten points in fourteen service games. As the *Daily Star*'s headline writer put it, Murray had been "Kicked in the Nads." (Oh, behave!) In the aftermath, Murray was commendably realistic, sounding less like a crestfallen loser than a gushing movie reviewer offering breathless bites of praise for the performance he'd just witnessed:

"He hits the heaviest shot in tennis." — Andy Murray

"The ball jumps at a tough angle, something that I think Federer sometimes struggles with against him." — Andy Murray

"His forehand is just ridiculous." — Andy Murray

Most gratifying to Nadal, all of his adjustments to grass had been paying off. "Standing on top of the baseline and not two meters behind it," he was able to dictate play. Unlike past years, he was playing aggressively and proactively from the first ball in the rally. He was serving crisply. "It's been a good tournament so far," Nadal admitted with an indifferent shrug. But then he quickly added: "I have won nothing yet."

After the Murray match, Carlos Costa began nagging his client to shave. Costa explained that on Saturday Nadal was supposed to tape a video message for the Spanish bank Banesto, one of his sponsors. Nadal couldn't address his benefactors looking like a scraggly Ibiza beach bum. A creature of habit (and superstition), Nadal demurred.

With the field pared to four players, Federer and Nadal were one round removed from meeting in the Wimbledon final for a third straight year. In the semifinals Federer faced a player who'd been blessed with similarly generous amounts of raw talent: Marat Safin of Russia. Unlike Federer, however, Safin had been profligate with his gifts. Pete Sampras once described Safin's game as "the tennis of the future," and to his credit, Safin did win two Majors and attain the No. 1 ranking. He has also proven singularly adept at blazing self-destruction, an ability to go for months without winning a match. By his mid-twenties, he was tennis's lovably eccentric cast member, still capable of some scene-stealing roles — he won his second Major, the 2005 Australian Open, beating Federer along the way—but equally capable of disappearing for entire seasons. He entered Wimbledon ranked No. 75, yet he played top-tier tennis for six matches. At age twenty-eight, he'd grown resigned to his fate. "I'm pleased with the way things are going. But if I'm honest, I'd prefer to have the career of Federer," he explained with a sigh. "I'm tired of making comebacks."

Two hours after eating a plate of tagliatelle pasta and a banana for lunch, Federer snapped on his gloves and turned in a surgical performance. He broke Safin at the first opportunity, won the opening set in twenty-four minutes, and generally cruised from there. Federer had a few lapses, going "off the boil," as the Brits say, and overcooking a few shots. But he conjured up his best tennis, including a silken running backhand flick up the line, and prevailed in straight sets to reach yet another final. Afterward he betrayed some of his sensitivity to having his supremacy questioned. Asked if it might help him to challenge for his sixth straight Wimbledon as something other than the overwhelming favorite, Federer said sharply, "Look . . . I'm on an incredible winning streak on grass. First somebody has to be able to break that, you know, before we start talking differently."

As Federer finished off Safin, Nadal prepared for his match against Germany's Rainer Schuettler by warming up with John McEnroe. It made for a great photo op and video clip, and if hitting with a forty-nine-year-old lefty wasn't necessarily the ideal way to regroove your strokes before facing a thirty-two-year-old righty, it hardly mattered. Schuettler is one of those tennis players who would probably have been a formidable talent a generation ago, a solidly built speed demon with excellent returns of serve. But in A.D. 2008, a player who does everything capably but lacks a real weapon is consigned to journeyman status. Though he once briefly inhabited the top 5, Schuettler entered the tournament barely in the top 100; but he won five matches, registering one of the better results of his career. To his credit, he did not capitulate in the semifinals and did not turn in one of those happy-to-have-gotten-this-far-now-where-do-I-pick-up-my-check? performances. He needed to be beaten. Nadal obliged.

So it was that Federer-Nadal XVIII — the "Dream Wimbledon Final," as the BBC billed it — was set. All but two players had been sifted out of the draw. Illustrative of most big tournaments during the Federer-Nadal axis, the pretenders were left to keep pretending; the dark horses stayed dark; the also-rans also ran; the Cinderellas wore tattered clothes and missed the grand ball.

Both players tried to relax as much as possible the day before the match. They both had massages and played cards and watched television at their respective houses. At his marble-topped dining room table, Nadal wolfed down the same meal of pasta with shrimp sauce and mushrooms he'd been eating throughout the tournament. (Habit, remember, not superstition.)

On the day of reckoning, Sunday, July 6, Federer arrived at the club first, at around 10:30, and Nadal came half an hour or so later for a cursory hitting session. Federer had recruited Bradley Klahn, a junior player from California who was headed to Stanford in the fall and, most important, a lefty able to mimic Nadal's style. To keep the Centre Court grass pristine for the final, players are forbidden to warm up on the court before the match, so Federer was dispatched to Court 17.

Nadal chose to practice with Costa, his agent, on Court 19. As Nadal, nervous, struggled to keep the ball in the court, Costa noticed that he had finally performed some grounds-keeping on his face, taking a razor to his stubble for the first time in the tournament. Costa was thrilled that Nadal would look presentable when he taped that message for the Spanish bank. Oh, no, said Nadal, his decision to shave wasn't based on that. Flatly and without boasting, he explained, "When you win Wimbledon, you want to look your best."

First Set

6–4

IT WAS 14:37 LOCAL TIME when Federer tossed a Slazenger-brand ball up into the stark sky, inaugurating the 2008 Wimbledon men's final. The serve is the most important shot in tennis, the one stroke that is self-generated, hit irrespective of the opponent. It requires no reaction. Tennis's scoring system assumes that players will hold their serves, and that the player breaking serve once will achieve the two-game margin necessary to win a set.

While Federer has never set any speed records, he uses his serve to devastating effect. Uncoiling his body in perfect synchronicity, he genuflects and then thrusts his legs and surges upward and outward. His right arm extended, he meets the ball a few rows above the center of his strings, maybe two-thirds up the racket, and then whips across it, fusing his power with spin. Particularly when coupled with accuracy, the ball is intensely difficult to return.

For the entire tournament, Federer had been dialing in his serve. Before the final, he had delivered eighty-six aces — more than fourteen per match on average — and had double-faulted just four times. (Most mortals would be content with a 2:1 ratio. In fact, a random sample of 250 ATP matches reveals

that the average is 1.75:1.) In the eighteen previous sets Federer
had won at Wimbledon, his serve had been broken just twice.
Consider: in the French Open final four Sundays earlier, Nadal had broken Federer's serve three times in the final set alone.
Federer was trafficking in the obvious when he asserted that
he'd need to serve well to beat Nadal. But that didn't make it
any less true.

Federer's first serve of the match ticked the soft net, activat-
ing a sensor. Like a neuron firing, a light flashed on the keypad
of the chair umpire. "Let," said Pascal Maria, almost instanta-
neously. Federer hit the oxymoronic "second first serve," at 113
mph, deep to Nadal's backhand. The ball appeared destined
to strafe past Nadal. But at the last possible interval, he flung
the ball back over the net into Federer's court. And the rally
was on. Twenty-five years earlier, when John McEnroe played
Ivan Lendl in the Wimbledon semifinals, only one point in
the whole match lasted more than six strokes. Further evidence to support the claim that the pace on Wimbledon grass
was much slower than it had once been, on the very first point
of their match Nadal and Federer engaged in a protracted,
punch-counterpunch exchange.

On the fourteenth stroke of the rally, Nadal chased a ball
deep in the corner and rocketed a forehand, laced with his singular blend of power and spin. The ball flew over the middle of
the doubles alley for much of its flight. Then, like an airplane
on autopilot, it hooked and descended in the corner of the
singles court, maybe six inches from both lines, out of Federer's reach. This was the kind of point that gets played deep in a
match when both players are "feeling" the ball and have found
their rhythm. No match starts out with a fourteen-stroke exchange that ends with an are-you-kidding-me? winner. It was
one point of 412 to follow, but it presaged beautifully what
was to come. It was Ivan Lendl who once remarked, "There

are two important points in tennis, the first one and the last one." Well, the first one went to Nadal.

Nadal reacted with a slight fist pump and a request for a towel, pleased with both the actual shot and the emphatic early message it sent. Federer looked into the strings of his racket, betraying no emotion. An inauspicious beginning, perhaps. But it was just one point. Indeed, on the next exchange, Nadal overhit a forehand beyond the baseline and, quickly, it was 15 all. Such is the inherent cruelty of tennis. One instant you play a well-constructed point, capped by a sensational winner. The next instant you commit a careless error, missing a shot by a few inches. And everything is offset, the score back to being tied.

Federer next hit a slicing serve that Nadal struggled to handle. The return was a meek offering that bounced inside the service line. Federer approached and hooked a one-hand backhand that Nadal retrieved but was unable to maneuver back over the net. Nothing fancy, but clinical, aggressive tennis. 30–15. Federer then controlled an eleven-stroke rally, improving his position incrementally with each shot, finishing with a forehand winner. He ended the game with a 129 mph ace, his fastest serve of the day.

Though Nadal's serve might be the weakest component of his game—at worst it's functional, at best it's effective—it's also the most improved. Nadal's first year at Wimbledon, his average serve traveled at 99 mph; this year, his serves were cutting the air faster than 115 mph on average. Playing at a glacially slow pace, he bounces the ball as many as a dozen times before beginning a straightforward, mechanical motion. Even with Nadal's muscular legs and powerful left arm, his serves seldom exceed 120 mph. (For comparison: when Venus Williams won the Wimbledon women's title the previous afternoon, she clocked a 129 mph serve.) But Nadal's renderings come adorned with all manner of spin, and especially when they dart out wide, they can be a challenge to return.

Nadal's first serve of the day was a cutter to Federer's backhand that landed fortuitously on a clump of dirt. The ball bounced erratically and ticked off Federer's racket. Federer is a firm believer in karmic tennis justice. Tennis luck — the bad bounces and the questionable line calls — he's often said, evens out over the course of a match. Without pausing to express disappointment, Federer walked laterally to return the next serve, positioning himself a yard behind the sideline.

Over the next few points, both players would reveal some of their strategy for the match. Nadal cut every serve to Federer's backhand, an attempt to play to Federer's weaker return wing and open up the court. Federer may have been obligated to hit backhand returns, but once he got a forehand, he was going to belt it — take a "big cut," in the vernacular — and head netward. At 0–15, Federer scrambled to retrieve a pair of Nadal zinging forehands, but worked his way back in position and knocked off an oil painting of a forehand volley.

Easier said than done, granted, but it was a primer for how Federer could beat Nadal: engage him, deny him rhythm, attack prudently, then tap the genius. Plenty of ink has been spilled (and the digital equivalent) expounding on how Nadal vexes Federer as no other player does. But the reverse is true too. Nadal knows that Federer is the only player capable of beating him on sheer talent alone, and volleys like the one Federer had just executed were a vivid reminder.

As the sun strained to poke through the clouds, Nadal responded with more effective serves directed to Federer's backhand. He held handily for 1–1. As in boxing, this was the "feeling out" phase, both combatants easing their way into the contest.

Nadal would later explain that if he could neutralize Federer's serve and get into a backcourt rally, he'd better his chances. In the third game, shortening his swing to respond to Federer's offerings, Nadal applied pressure with his returns. At 30–30, he won a baseline exchange when Federer missed a routine backhand, gifting Nadal an early break point. Federer spun a second serve conservatively into the middle of the box. Nadal took a step to his right and put his full weight into an inside-out backhand. The ball alighted in the corner. Federer practically whiffed. The ball shot off his frame, not his strings, and landed in the crowd, a legacy of Nadal's devastating spin.

The match was ten minutes old and Nadal had notched a service break, "drawing first blood," as broadcasters in a variety of tongues predictably put it. It was the first plot point. Watching Nadal bully Federer recalled A. J. Liebling's description of the great Archie Moore getting pummeled by a less artistic foe. Like Moore, Federer was the opera singer being "crowded off the stage by a guy who can only shout."

Nadal jogged enthusiastically to his chair. Federer skulked to his. In the players' box, a dozen heads nodded in unison in the manner of bobblehead dolls. The six Federer supporters in the front row conveyed the message: *It's okay. Break him back.* With the same gesture, the six Nadal supporters conveyed the opposite: *That's it. Keep it up.*

The forced intimacy foisted on Federer and Nadal extended to their respective entourages. At every junior sporting event — peewee soccer, Little League baseball, junior tennis — those with opposing rooting interests naturally situate themselves on opposite sides of the field, court, or rink. Yet at Wimbledon, the supporters share the same cramped box in the court's southeast corner, the higher seed's contingent in the front row, the lower seed's contingent behind them. The seating arrangement borders on cruel: as if it's not stressful enough

to watch your child/lover/client compete in a high-stakes contest, imagine doing so with the opponent's representatives
seated alongside you. At the same time, there's a certain civility
to it. If the two sets of fans with the greatest emotional investment can sit beside each other in peace, well, you should be
able to behave yourself too.

It turned out that the six seats in the players' box could
accommodate only a small portion of the Nadal entourage,
many of whom had flown in from Majorca that morning. The
"Rafaelites" numbered more than twenty and included all four
grandparents, uncles, aunts, friends, the professional golfer
Gonzalo Fernandez-Castaño, and the head of the Real Madrid
soccer club. Seating was so tight that Nadal's parents, Sebastian
and Ana Maria Parera, were made to sit in an overflow section.
Other family members, including the grandparents, were scattered throughout the venue in spare seats. Team Federer was
smaller. From left to right: agent, mother, girlfriend, the ubiq-
uitous Gwen Stefani and Gavin Rossdale, and father.

Settling into their seats before the match, the two camps
exchanged handshakes and pleasantries. Federer's father, Robert—a sturdily built, genial man with a head of gray hair and a
black mustache who resembles a small-town butcher—broke
the tension when he offered warm handshakes all around.
He'd met most of the Nadal clan before, and though there was
a language barrier, he'd always been quite fond of them. During the match, they sat mostly in silence, murmuring among
themselves, careful not to cheer uninhibitedly and offend the
other side.

The other 14,988 or so spectators were considerably louder
and more engaged. The previous day, when Venus Williams
had defeated her younger sister, Serena, in the women's final,
the Centre Court crowd had been subdued, clapping with-

out necessarily cheering. Appreciative, yes, but also conflicted. Who, after all, cheers for one sister to beat the other? The match had the slightly hollow feel of an exhibition, as there was a surfeit of spectacular shotmaking but a deficit of that other ingredient vital for a seminal sporting event: tension.

Now the crowd betrayed a much different personality. Perhaps because neither player is remotely offensive, Federer and Nadal don't cleave public opinion the way most rivals do. Still, their differences are sufficiently stark that most fans clearly prefer one to the other. Particularly when Federer and Nadal play a match for world domination. At some level, it becomes a personality test: do you root for the proud, wounded champion to defend his honor or for the relentless underdog to topple him? The graceful sorcerer or the indefatigable artisan? As it was, fans' rhythmic cheers of "Rajah, Rajah" were countered with "Rafa, Rafa." For every unfurled Spanish flag there was an equivalent Swiss banner. The place crackled with electricity. There is, as they say, a wisdom of crowds. And on this day, after just a few games of play, there was a collective sense that this was going to be a special match.

Here's what else helped the ambience: Wimbledon is in many ways a people's event. The tournament's image, of course, is one of almost comical elitism. At "the Championships"—as Wimbledon immodestly calls itself, as though no other tennis tournaments of note exist—all those British patricians, who might otherwise be foxhunting in the countryside, park their Aston Martins and Land Rovers at a private club and watch tennis played on a lawn. Though there is an undeniable current of money and class—we're hard-pressed to name other sporting events that serve tea on a balcony during breaks in the action or post Kipling verses on the portal to the playing surface—for every ascot and sundress there's a fan wearing a rainbow wig or a pair of novelty sunglasses. For every Brahmin there's a bloke.

For one thing, the event passes up almost incalculable revenue in order to protect what a club member calls "the Wimbledon fan experience." When organizers investigated the feasibility of constructing the Centre Court roof, they were told it would be cheaper to build an entirely new structure than to install a retractable canopy on a stadium that opened in 1922. Too bad, the club replied; Wimbledon without Centre Court wouldn't be Wimbledon. At the preposterous expense of, we're told, more than $400 million, the new roof will cover the old edifice.

This expense could be subsidized at least partially by naming rights (HSBC Centre Court?) and signage (say, a blue and red British Airways logo behind the court) and luxury boxes. These revenue rivers have become so common in the American sportscape one scarcely pays them any mind. But if such crass commercialism might bring in millions, it might also corrupt the "fan experience." At Wimbledon there are no proper suites and no naming rights. The only logos visible on Centre Court, subtle ones at that, are the Rolex scoreboard, the Slazenger ball receptacle, the IBM insignia on the service speed board, and a small, crusty decal behind the umpire's chair for Robinson's brand of barley water, perhaps the most vile drink on earth, incidentally.

Compare this to Arthur Ashe Stadium, the main site of the U.S. Open in New York. The walls behind the baseline feature the logos of Olympus, JPMorgan Chase, usopen.org, and the USTA. Courtside doorways advertise Heineken Premium Light. Over the doubles alley, a pair of plastic Chase Bank logos the size of hubcaps have, in a true feat of embroidery, been sewn into the net. The umpire's chair and courtside umbrellas are slathered with a logo for Continental Airlines. Courtside tubs advertise Wilson, Gatorade, and Evian. IBM sponsors the service speed clock, while Citizen provides the official time. (Presumably, for the right price the unofficial time is available for sponsorship.) The ball kids wear Polo Ralph Lauren, the horse logo on the back of their shirts approaching the size of a small pony. The line judges, also clad from head to toe in Polo, are stationed behind wooden Polo placards on the court. The sidelines signage heralds Lexus, American Express, Valspar paints, Mass Mutual, and George Foreman — the brand of the popular grill, one assumes, and not the retired heavyweight boxer himself. Directly above the stadium's ninety — *ninety* — corporate suites are additional signs for sponsors: Tiffany, the *New York Times,* Evian, CBS Sports, Lever 2000, *Tennis* magazine, Grey Goose vodka, Lu biscuits, Canon, and Juvéderm injectable gel. At least that was the inventory taken on Heineken Night. It might have been slightly different on Juvéderm Day or Evian Natural Spring Water Day.

The Wimbledon ticketing policy is also surprisingly democratic. First dibs on the seats go to the All England Club's 500 members and the 2,300 debenture holders who have paid upward of $50,000 for the right to buy tickets. The remaining tickets are sold to the public at an average price of £87 ($170 in the summer of 2008) — not cheap, but hardly exorbitant. (Average Super Bowl ticket on the secondary market: $3,000.) For the first five rounds, the tournament allocates 500 first-come first-served Centre Court seats for "queuers," who camp out in a field a mile from the club, wake up the next morning, and stand on line. The queuers include the likes of Blake Eddie, a stubbly twenty-nine-year-old from Newcastle who wanted to see Federer play. He cashed in some British Airways frequent-flier miles, jetted to Heathrow, took a bus to Wimbledon, camped out, stood in the queue, and spent £75 for a ticket that put him six rows back of the court. "I'd spend just as much going to a concert or a music festival," he says. "And I wouldn't be near as close. I mean, I got to see Federer live. On Centre Court of Wimbledon!"

It's sports' answer to noblesse oblige. The tournament could easily make the tickets available through an on-line brokerage such as stubhub.com and fetch ten times the prices it receives selling directly to the commoner. But that, too, would corrupt the fan experience. Besides, the payoff comes in other ways. The stands of other big-time sporting events are filled with corporate stiffs and the Brie-eating, see-and-be-seen luxury-box set.* Wimbledon gets authentic sports fans.

As Nadal prepared to serve at 2–1, he reached behind his waist and tugged at the posterior crease of his shin-length clamdiggers. It's a regrettable habit that traces back to his junior days and in recent years has provoked a fair amount of mockery. Novak Djokovic lampooned this tic when he performed an impersonation of Nadal, earning himself a permanent spot in the Nadal doghouse. Several members of the British press have coined Nadal "the Knicker Picker." This habit is also something other than a ringing endorsement for the comfort of the Nike apparel that he is paid to wear. Nadal grows understandably embarrassed when asked about this tic, claiming that it's unconscious, and though he's tried to quit, he's helpless to do anything about it. Unseemly as this habit is, it's also weirdly endearing. At a time when athletes are meticulously marketed —some, including Andy Murray, keep an image consultant

---

* The French Open semifinal matches often begin in front of pastures of empty seats. Why? Because the sessions coincide with lunchtime, and what ticket holder wants to watch tennis when there is catered *déjeuner* in the BNP Paribas hospitality suite?

on the payroll—there's something to be said for a global superstar who picks his ass in public.

When Nadal managed to disengage his hand from his shorts, he commenced one of the more entertaining games of the match. He took a 40–0 lead with three winners, one more dazzling than the next. Federer then rallied to deuce, pressuring Nadal with relentlessly deep balls to the backhand side, followed by an approach to the net. After Nadal hit a wayward hooking forehand at deuce, Federer held a break point. It was the typical "big point," as they say in tennis-speak, an opportunity for Federer to even the match. Predictably, Nadal kicked a second serve to Federer's backhand. After another hard-hitting baseline exchange, Federer drove a routine forehand long by half a foot or so. This epitomized the maddening nature of facing Nadal, a player whose defensive skills are so exceptional, the opponent feels pressured to attempt low-margin shots, imprudent risks he wouldn't ordinarily undertake. Federer's shoulders slumped and his head drooped. After a few more deuces and a few more knicker picks, Nadal served out the game. Danger averted.

Federer responded with a game that resembled Wii tennis. He simply placed the ball wherever he pleased, holding serve at love, winning four points in fifty seconds. *If only it were always this easy.*

It was hard not to notice that after three service games, Federer had yet to serve-and-volley. Once considered *the* tactic for success on grass courts, serve-and-volley tennis has come to resemble a once popular dance step that has fallen out of vogue. The often-quoted statistic: in the 2002 final—the last final before the Era of Federer—neither Lleyton Hewitt nor David Nalbandian played serve-and-volley tennis on a single point. You only had to survey the topography of the Centre Court lawn to see how unhip serve-and-volleying had become. The baseline resembled a grazed savanna, a few blades of green sticking out of the brown dirt; the area around the net remained a pristine lawn, seemingly untouched by human feet. Clay court masters who once begged off Wimbledon altogether were suddenly reaching the later rounds. Nadal's success on grass is merely the apotheosis.

Assessing the evidence, most investigators reached the logical conclusion that the Wimbledon grass was somehow thicker or denser and thus playing slower than it had it previous years. This slow grass blunted the speed of the ball, enabled the balls to bounce higher, and in turn discouraged serve-and-volleying. The BBC undertook a study that tracked two 126 mph serves that Federer had hit on Centre Court, one from 2003 and one from 2008. The 2003 serve traveled 52 mph by the time it had bounced on the grass and reached the returner; the 2008 serve traveled only 43 mph when it arrived. This study may have been junk science — unless the balls were directed to the exact same location with the same trajectory, the speed and bounce are irrelevant to gauging court speed — but nevertheless most observers could agree that *something* was up. A few players went so far as to assert that Wimbledon's courts currently play slower than the *clay* courts at the French Open.

Not so, replies Eddie Seaward, Wimbledon's head groundsman, a dignified, soft-spoken man in his mid-sixties who is surely the world's best-dressed horticulturist. Absently fiddling with his silk tie while maintaining his innocence, Seaward adamantly claims that he and his minions have done nothing to slow the grass, contrary to what players and fans — "my millions of unpaid consultants," he wryly calls them — believe. Seaward explains that for decades the Wimbledon lawns had been blanketed by a combination of perennial ryegrass and ominously named creeping fescue. In 2001, the club changed to 100 percent ryegrass, a strand known for its durability. "We needed to keep up with the modern game," Seaward says. "It had gotten so physical."

The task of maintaining the grass on the complex's thirty-nine courts falls to the staff of fourteen full-time greenskeepers and fourteen temporary hires. Days after the men's final, the club receives its shipment of ryegrass seed—imported from elsewhere in Europe—for the next year's event. The crew rips up the old court and removes any lateral growth and worms that might come to the surface when the courts dry. They re-seed the lawn and for the next eleven months the grass is allowed to mature naturally and is mowed to fourteen millimeters, the equivalent of a five o'clock shadow. During the tournament, it's trimmed to eight millimeters, the same length as always, Seaward says.

Seaward has two theories to explain the perception that the grass is playing slower and serve-and-volleying is an increasingly rare tactic: (1) Players have heard all the murmuring and now have almost "a mental thing," a low-grade paranoia, that the returners have an advantage. (2) If the courts are playing slower, it's not because of the grass but because of the soil underfoot. He and his men have packed it in a bit tighter in order to reduce wear and tear on the courts. And it's been hardened further as a result of unusually dry and warm weather. (Until the final match of the 2008 tournament, rain had rarely been a factor at Wimbledon.) The global warming and climate change that affect so much on our planet? It's having an impact on Wimbledon too.

Another swap of service holds made it 4–3, and by now both players were *in* the match. The knots in their stomachs had untied. Their hearts were no longer thumping away inside their chests. Their spigots of cortisol—the stress hormone that acts to relieve pain and discomfort but also breaks down muscle tissue—had been turned off. Had you looked closely at the players' eyes, you'd likely have seen that their pupils were no longer dilated. In short, as Federer and Nadal had settled into the match, fight-or-flight had given way to rest-and-digest. The sympathetic nervous system had ended its shift, replaced by the parasympathetic nervous system.

And that went for all three men on the court. Just as this was a defining match for Federer and Nadal, the same held true for Pascal Maria, the Frenchman who sat inconspicuously in the umpire's chair, tennis's wheeled throne. As with the players, this match marked a career milestone for Maria, a goal achieved, a reward for all the years of toil and trouble that preceded it. He, too, had gone through his prematch routine, much of it focused on suppressing the urge to urinate in the middle of the match. (That morning, he passed up his customary double espresso and peed at least ten times.) He, too, had invited family members to fly to London, sit courtside, and share the occasion. He wore a special outfit, a white, collared shirt and Wimbledon tie layered with a cable-stitch tennis sweater and blue blazer. Fortunately, no one was risking heatstroke on this day.

Maria, who was thirty-five, grew up in Nice. A tennis fanatic as a kid, he favored stylists like Stefan Edberg or players like Ivan Lendl and Mats Wilander who'd ruled the French Open. At sixteen, he wrenched his knee and couldn't play tennis for two years. His passion for the sport was such that he still watched teammates from his tennis club play their matches. At one interclub match, he was conscripted into duty. "Hey, Pascal, there's no umpire on one of the courts. You know tennis. Can you help us out?" With his bum knee, he clambered into the chair. Instantly he'd found his calling. Here was a way to sustain his intimacy with tennis. And in keeping with his personality, he could become a Keeper of Order, an Arbiter of Fair Play.

Mirroring the arc of an aspiring tennis player, Maria graduated from district events to French national events to low-level professional events. He had all the prerequisites for the official's job: a love of tennis, an eye for detail, a high threshold for waiting, a willingness to sublimate his ego. He had good fortune on his side of the net too. Bruno Rebeuh, a longtime chair umpire, belonged to Maria's tennis club and was happy to act as a mentor. Plus, living in Nice, Maria was within easy driving distance of many events, including the venerable ATP tournament in Monte Carlo.

Maria was in his mid-twenties when he was asked to be a line judge at the 1996 Australian Open. By the age of thirty, he'd worked more than three hundred matches and was honored with a gold badge—the *ne plus ultra* among tennis officials—enabling him to land full-time jobs, first with the International Tennis Federation. Like most players, he has a preferred surface. "Clay, because it's what I grew up on," he says. But he doesn't mind grass. Though the ball travels faster and skids more, there's the benefit of the chalky titanium paste on the lines, a little white smoke signal indicating that the ball is inbounds. Not surprisingly, Maria cites the two hundred nights a year on the road as the chief occupational drawback. The great appeal? "I have a ticket to the best matches in the world."

There's both an art and a science to chair umpiring, but it mostly comes down to striking a balance. The job entails being an authority without being authoritarian and knowing the players intimately—their games, their dispositions, their personality quirks, their tempos—without really knowing them at all. (To avoid the appearance of bias, there are strict rules against off-court fraternizing with the athletes, no matter how often you see them in hotel lobbies or departure lounges.) Chair umpires must be an integral part of the match without insinuating themselves into the show. "In most jobs, the more people that know your name, the better you're probably doing," says Maria. "In this job it's the opposite. You're in public but the goal is to be invisible."

Maria and his few dozen colleagues take pains to achieve this. They dress in identical uniforms and often obscure their faces with caps. They're usually barred by their superiors from granting interviews and seldom stop to socialize with fans as they leave the court. Most of them are physically unremarkable — Maria is handsome in a simple way, a man of average height and average build with close-cropped hair. (Not coincidentally, the one occasionally recognized umpire is Norm Chryst, who sports a glistening bald head and a glistening earring.) Comprising a sort of secret society, the officials keep to themselves at tournaments and often stay in a different hotel from the rest of the tennis caravan.

Apart from being intimately familiar with the rules, the best umpires, sedentary as they may be, are quick on their feet. Some carry a sewing kit onto the court in case a player wears a sponsor patch that exceeds regulation size and needs trimming. Others will use the pitch of their voice to quiet a rowdy crowd. Still others will use a pointed phrase to avoid an ugly confrontation with players. For instance, players will defer to the chair about a line call and ask, "Did you see it clearly?" If the umpire did, he or she — recently, and with little fanfare, women have been officiating more and more men's matches — might respond, "I saw the ball out" or "I saw the ball good." (Translation: Don't waste a replay challenge.) If not, he or she might respond, "It was too close for me to overrule." (Translation: This would be a good time to use a challenge.)

Like a top player, Maria breezed through his Wimbledon matches with little trouble. No drama. No complaints. No brain cramps such as the one his (now former) colleague famously suffered several years ago at Wimbledon when he mistakenly neglected to award Venus Williams a point she had rightfully won. Umpires are trained not to prioritize matches. They're there to watch the ball and uphold the rules, whether it's a first-round qualifier match on Court 20 or a Federer-Nadal Grand Slam final. But that lofty ideal resists human nature. And Maria knew that his strong tournament should at least put him in the running to sit in the chair for the men's final.

The assignment for the final was determined by a committee. The tournament referee, the supervisor, the chief of umpires, and the tournament board each put forth candidates. Competence during the previous rounds of the tournament was a factor. So was nationality. To avoid charges of bias, if the players are from different countries, you will never see a chair umpire of the same nationality as either competitor.*

When Pascal Maria got word that he would be overseeing his first Wimbledon final, he called his wife. Much as he tried to outwit himself by thinking this was just another match, he knew the reality: occupying the chair for the men's final at Wimbledon was, as he puts it, "the cream." No tennis fan, his wife seldom came to events and had never sat through an entire match. But he prevailed on her to leave their three-year-old daughter with the in-laws and fly to London. She relented,

---

* If, however, the players are from the same country, it's entirely possible —likely, even—that the chair umpire will also be a compatriot.

and ended up sitting courtside next to the substitute chair umpire, Carlos Ramos. After a few games, she knew she'd picked one hell of a first match to attend.

Sitting on their designated chairs during the changeovers between odd games, Nadal and Federer both took only small sips of water. Even in the mild conditions such as this day's, a tennis player can sweat off a few liters of fluid an hour, compared to five liters an hour when it's humid. Yet the body can only uptake two liters an hour. Ingest too much fluid and it hinders movement and breathing and induces nausea. Take in too little and you'll dehydrate. ATP trainers tell players that a four percent loss of body weight can result in a twenty percent loss of physical capabilities. Hydration is a delicate balance; players try to find it by coming onto the court fully hydrated and then resisting the temptation to guzzle even when they're most tired.

With a firm breeze swirling and shafts of sun throwing shadows off the court, Nadal served at 4–3 with new balls. Again he directed his delivery to Federer's backhand. By the end of the game, Nadal had hit twenty-five of his twenty-seven serves to Federer's backhand. A BBC radio commentator remarked, "That's what we'd come to expect from a lefty." The comment hung in the air unadorned, as though it needed no further explanation.

As is the case in most sports, a disproportionately large chunk of the great tennis players have been lefties, immortals on the order of Laver, McEnroe, Connors, Navratilova, and Seles. The influence of lefties has waned somewhat in recent years, but given that the dextral outnumber the sinistral nine to one in society at large, lefties are still well represented in tennis's top 100.

Though there's no consensus as to why lefties are so successful in sports, it's not for a lack of theories. Typically, lefties have stronger "off hands," which helps in such skills as batting and shooting a basketball—this would certainly describe Nadal, whose off hand is his true dominant hand. It's also been hypothesized that, in a world rigged for righties (have you ever tried buying a left-handed power saw?), lefties persist because of sharply honed survival instincts, which translate well to sports. There's also the whole left-brain/right-brain theory, according to which lefties are more creative and poised than righties.

Why have lefties thrived in tennis? It's been suggested that a left-handed grip enables a player to generate a "special spin," though physics types have been known to roll their eyes at this notion. Another theory: whereas righties naturally slice their serve to the left side of the opponent's service box, lefties' natural slice stroke sends the ball to the right side. So in the ad court, where most of the "big points" are played, lefties have a natural tendency to hook their serves out wide to their opponents' backhand (usually the weaker flank) and push them off the court. If righties serve out wide to the ad court, they are "kicking" the ball and not slicing it, a difficult shot that, geometrically, entails hitting the ball over the "highest" point of the net. Plus, once it bounces, it pops up rather than skids down. Got that?

Specific to Federer-Nadal, when Nadal hits his dive-bombing crosscourt forehand, he drives it to Federer's backhand, his weaker side. And, especially on slower surfaces, Nadal's spin-laden shots take that high bounce, putting Federer in the unenviable, defensive position of hitting a backhand—a one-handed backhand at that—at neck level.

It's also said that lefties are more prone to the sort of mental pliability that's helpful (necessary?) for tennis. As the astute

commentator Mary Carillo, herself a lefty, recently explained
to *Sports Illustrated*: "Mainly, we're nuts. You look at all the
lefthanders in tennis—Rod Laver was normal, but he was
Australian—and you've got some real wing nuts. Connors,
McEnroe, Goran Ivanisevic, Guillermo Vilas. You just love it
when you've got people like that representing your group in
tennis." What about Nadal? "That kid has a different spin on
how to construct points, develop a rally," she said. "He thinks
outside the box."

But maybe the best explanation is that lefties simply present a different, unsettling "look," with all those confounding
angles. Just as a righty boxer facing a southpaw needs to reverse his thinking (or else walk directly into a jab), the righty
tennis player is constantly recalibrating and then inverting the
conventional geometry. Federer, who's been playing lefties all
his life, seeks out left-handed practice partners before he plays
Nadal. As recently as 2007, Federer flew a young American
lefty, Jesse Levine, to his training base in Dubai (coach class,
since you asked) for a weeklong hitting session. In this, Federer's eighteenth career match against Nadal, he sometimes resembles the man driving on the unfamiliar side of the road.
Asked to describe Nadal's game, on a number of occasions
Federer has used the word "awkward." That adjective, coming
from a man who likes everything to be organized and logical,
is packed with meaning.

Before serving at 3–5 to stay in the set, Federer stood with his
back to the net, receiving the Slazenger balls from a solemn-
looking ball boy, examining them as if selecting a ripe melon
at the market. When he found the balls he liked, he kept one,
put a second in his pocket, and batted the reject back to the
kid. The ritual, undertaken by most players, serves twin purposes. One is practical: the more tennis balls are used, the more

fuzz they accumulate. The more fuzz, the more air resistance. The more air resistance, the more easily the ball is returned. So players, in effect, search for the freshest balls. (Which is the reason the first player to serve with new balls is seldom broken.) The other purpose: as players caress the tennis balls between points, they can steal a few seconds to collect themselves and take inventory of the match.

Federer won the game with ease. Now in rhythm, he seemed to be guiding his serves with a GPS. In the span of fifty seconds, he hit four unreturnable first serves to win the game at love, rendering Nadal a spectator. It was difficult to believe that Nadal had somehow earned that service break earlier in the set. Nevertheless, Federer walked to his chair trailing 4–5.

Whether it's because of Federer's dramatically wavy hair, his fastidious grooming, or his jet-setting-sophisticate persona, one tends to think of him as a dandy. But watching him up close, stalking around the court while projecting so much intensity, he can look genuinely rugged. With his flattened nose and small eyes set deep and close together, tucked under thick brows . . . well, give Federer a different haircut and a different outfit and it's easy to picture him, say, working the docks of Brooklyn. He is also decidedly more hirsute than most players. Nadal is among the many pro tennis players who clearly shave or wax excess arm and leg hair. Notionally, it's done to prevent infections that can occur in conjunction with massages and tapings, though one player suspects that "man-scaping" is sometimes practiced "for psychological reasons, so your muscles are being shown off."

When it comes to tactics, tennis players can resemble kids who make a joke, get the desired reaction, then go on telling the same joke for the rest of the afternoon. Yet again Nadal served into Federer's backhand. Though the placement was

predictable and Federer was in perfect position, he drove the
return wide. Federer, though, won the next two points, first
with defense, then with a cold-blooded backhand volley, a
piece of shotmaking so luxurious that it drew an impromptu
standing ovation in parts of the stadium. Winning a point so
emphatically also gave Federer an extra surge of satisfaction.
As he describes it, "Probably the most satisfying moment in
tennis is when you can close a point at the net. You feel like
the other guy was pressured because you were such a good athlete."

At 15–30, Federer drove a routine topspin backhand half
a foot beyond the baseline. Projecting disappointment— *You
can't friggin' miss those, Roger*—he took a few steps to his right
and then, as if suddenly remembering an errand he'd forgotten to run, raised his left hand. Immediately, Maria, the chair
ump, saw the signal and intoned: "Mr. Federer is challenging
the call on the right baseline." Everyone, including the players,
fixed their gaze on the scoreboard monitors at court level behind each baseline.

Since 2006, the questionable line calls that once triggered
heated arguments and lingering controversy now trigger video
review. Named for its founder, Paul Hawkins, who has a Ph.D.
in artificial intelligence, the Hawk-Eye ball-tracking system
represents tennis's most important technological advance since
the graphite racket. Though Hawkins's CV befits a professo-
rial type with a lab coat and hair sprouting from his ears, he's
an athletic-looking, sandy-haired Brit in his mid-thirties who
usually looks as if he's just played a round of golf. A sports
fan, Hawkins believed he could trace the precise flight of a
tennis ball by employing the same technology used for brain
surgery and missile tracking. His system uses ten small high-
definition cameras, spaced evenly around the court's perimeter—in this case, atop the Centre Court roof—to track the

ball. In a claustrophobia-inducing booth under the court's rafters, Hawkins watches the matches alongside ten computers,
each corresponding to one of the cameras.

When a player challenges a line call, each computer sends
a black-and-white image of the relevant call to a central computer. The computer then ties the ten images together and
produces a 3-D image, which is what fans see reproduced on
the video screen. This all transpires in a matter of seconds. At
some events, Hawkins has been instructed to delay the production for a few more seconds to add to the drama. (This at
a time when other sports, notably the NFL, are wary of replay
technology because it is too time-consuming to administer.)

The rub: Hawk-Eye does not show where the ball actually
lands. Using computer modeling and a complex algorithm, the
system reconstructs the *probable* path of the ball. As Hawkins
puts it, "Hawk-Eye doesn't show what really happened, but
it shows what was statistically likely to have happened—to a
very, very accurate degree." The International Tennis Federation rules state that an electronic line-calling system must be
able to judge a ball in or out within 5 millimeters; Hawk-Eye's
margin of error averages 3.6 millimeters.

Hawk-Eye has been a resounding success. It's improved accuracy and ended the suspicion that the outcomes of matches
have been determined, or at least influenced, by dubious line
calls. One of the initial concerns was that Hawk-Eye would
bleach the color from the sport, obviating those famous McEn-
roevian tirades (as if this were a bad thing). Though players,
now armed with recourse, no longer blow a gasket arguing
with officials, they still show their character based on how and
when they deploy their allotment of three replay challenges per
set. Hawk-Eye is popular with the crowds in the stands—"fan
friendly," as they say—and the television audience. The officials, told to discharge their duties "as they would were Hawk-

Eye not in existence," are thankful for the "backup." Happy
for the peace of mind, the players like it too.

One of the few vocal critics has been Federer. A staunch tra-
ditionalist, he at first dismissed Hawk-Eye as a gimmick when
it was unveiled in 2006. (As Mats Wilander once explained it,
"Of course Federer is conservative. If you had his record, you
wouldn't want to see anything change either. You'd want things
to stay exactly the way they were!") Deep in the 2007 Wimbledon final, Nadal hit a shot that, to the naked eye, appeared
out of bounds by a fair margin. Federer stopped play, and the
umpire agreed the ball was out. Television replays seemed to
confirm it. Nadal challenged the call, and Hawk-Eye indicated
that it was in. Federer went nuts—at least by his decorous
standards—declaring that Hawk-Eye was "killing" him. To no
avail, he demanded, "Turn it off!" Hawkins stands by that call,
asserting that the ball was in by one millimeter and the naked
eye was deceived because the ball compresses when it hits the
court. "Broadcast cameras aren't that accurate," he says confi-
dently. "People believe it because they're seeing real pictures as
opposed to the virtual world."

Hawk-Eye persists. Federer remains a skeptic. He uses the
technology, but it appears that he often challenges calls not
because he disagrees—in many cases he'll already have moved
to the opposite side of the court, expecting to be proven
wrong—but because it's a way of channeling some of his anger. He'll miss a shot, challenge the call, and transfer his frustration with himself onto that stupid contraption.

Such was the case here, it seemed. The fans watched as a
representation of the ball appeared on the screen, leaving a yellow comet tail and landing a good half foot beyond the baseline. *Oh, well.* Federer ran his left hand through his hair and
hunched over to return serve at 30–30.

Nadal set up his first set point with a punishing inside-out forehand he punctuated with a cry of "*Vamos!*" Federer responded by setting up Nadal with creative, sharply angled strokes and finishing off the point with a snapping one-handed backhand. (Reporter's notes: sick set-up and d/own-line, b/h crowd goes crzy,,, .. gutsy shot 2 sv set pt.) Federer then stormed the net and put away a forehand volley. Suddenly Federer had a break point to even the match. In his box, Federer's retinue cheered enthusiastically. Gavin Rossdale leaned forward, clenching his fist in the air.

Nadal responded. When Federer attacked the net, Nadal whipped a passing shot that Federer batted long. His sense of timing exquisite, Nadal then hit his first ace of the day to give himself another set point. Federer countered, driving Nadal off the court with a series of potent forehands and setting up this third break point after another series of baseline tracer fire. This baseline badinage, this thrust and parry, this street fighting on the crucial points enthralled the crowd.

Then, as is so often the case in tennis, the battle shifted from the physical to the mental front. Nadal spun in an innocuous 91 mph second serve to Federer's backhand. Inexplicably, Federer dumped a weak return into the net, spinning and throwing back his head with frustration as the ball came to rest. With that squandered opportunity clearly lodged in his head, Federer missed another backhand on the deuce point. On Nadal's third set point, he played four straight balls to Federer's backhand. On the fourth, Federer jerked his body a split second too early. This lapse in technique and concentration caused him to drive the ball into the net once again. "Game and first set. Nadal. Six games to four."

Second Set

6–4

THERE WAS A TIME not all that long ago, during the Tennis Boom, when the professional tour was populated mostly by Americans and Australians, with the odd Swede, Argentine, or Czech thrown in. The circuit threaded its way through the United States, where the ATP was headquartered and the vital decisions were made. American television ratings, then the ultimate sports barometer, were robust. Tennis was in many ways an American sport, open to the rest of the world.

When economists need a vivid illustration of both the promise and the peril of globalization, they could do worse than study professional tennis in its contemporary state. The sport is now played, watched, and followed by more people than ever. By most measures, it's never been healthier. So far this decade, every continent, save Antarctica, has been represented in the top 10. The pro events that were once held in Dallas and Scottsdale and Chicago have moved to such outposts as Dubai, Shanghai, Bangkok, and Chennai. Now based in London, the ATP also has offices in Florida, Monte Carlo, and Sydney. In passive PowerPoint-speak: the labor pool has deepened, markets have been penetrated, the brand has been built. Tennis is *everywhere*. There's a conciliatory saying in other American sports when a team, say, misses a last-second field goal or loses a baseball game in the bottom of the ninth inning: "There are a billion people in China who don't care." In tennis, those billion people in China — at least an appreciable percentage of them — really *do* care.

If global expansion has benefited the sport overall, there's no denying that an accompanying dilution has hurt the sport in the United States, where tennis has retreated to niche status, somewhere between golf and horseracing. Parochial by nature, the American sports public has an easier time rooting for John, Jimmy, and Andy than for all those Guillermos and Yevgenys. (Consider that the most popular American sport, NFL football, is the least diluted by globalization.) The practical effects of globalization have also hurt tennis in the United States. There are language barriers. There are steep travel costs. There are time differences — the PGA golf tour usually spans three time zones, ideal for television; the ATP spans the globe. Perhaps above all, it's hard for American fans to build a relationship with tennis players who seldom compete on American soil. The obligatory Tiger Woods comparison: provided he's healthy, Woods will play between sixteen and twenty events in the United States in a year's time. Roger Federer is lucky to play four events in the United States. American tennis fans who complain that the sport is dying have it wrong. Tennis isn't dying at all; it's just moving offshore.

As a result, compelling theater though it might be, the Federer-Nadal rivalry has struggled to gain traction among mainstream American sports fans. To them, it takes on the same dimensions as soccer. Or even opera. *I know I'm supposed to like it, but it's so damn foreign, it doesn't do it for me.* His premise may have been disagreeable, but Bill Simmons, the popular espn.com writer, spoke for Joe American Sports Fan when he wrote a column on the eve of the 2008 Wimbledon.

Prophetic in a way, Simmons addressed tennis's diminishing profile in the United States:

> If I guaranteed you that the 2008 Wimbledon men's final would be the best tennis match of the past 20 years, would you watch it? Amazingly, many sports fans would say no. Maybe they'd flick over to NBC a few times to "monitor the action." Maybe they'd swing by for the fifth set . . . But I don't have a single friend who'd watch four hours of tennis on a Sunday morning and, I'm guessing, neither do you. Unlike golf, another time-sucking sport that appeals to a specific audience, tennis lacks a Tiger to keep it relevant. When tennis develops its own version of Tiger—first Pete Sampras, then Roger Federer—the guys do almost more damage than good. We see the best tennis stars as the Ping-Pong player at a family gathering who destroys all the uncles and cousins, and eventually kills everyone's interest in playing Ping-Pong for the day. Golf is a sport that hinges on luck and timing, streaks and slumps, and the quirks of different courses. So it's almost inconceivable for a golfer to dominate as Tiger has. But for Federer to dominate, it's completely conceivable. And boring.

The thesis was open to debate. Tennis lacks quirks? The first Sunday in June, Federer and Nadal had played on crushed brick in Paris; the first Sunday in July, they were playing on Wimbledon's grass, a surface that can be ruined by the urine of a female fox. Federer's domination is boring? Maybe the outcomes of his matches are seldom in doubt, but the drama resides in how his genius will manifest itself. Federer is like the best mystery novel: you read it even though you know in advance how it will end. And isn't hegemony preferable to parity anyway? Men's tennis went through a period of anyone-can-beat-anyone, and it was a disaster. Between 1999 and 2003, ten different players enjoyed a stay in the rankings penthouse, sometimes for as brief a period as a week. When Carlos Moya,

Yevgeny Kafelnikov, Lleyton Hewitt, Juan Carlos Ferrero, and other less than transcendent figures were batting the top ranking back and forth, fans (to say nothing of ATP executives) would have contemplated a return to wooden rackets had it yielded a superpower, much less two.

Yet Simmons's column successfully captured popular perceptions about tennis in the United States. For all their success and geniality and good-guyness, neither Federer nor Nadal had ever been on the cover of *Sports Illustrated.* They had not starred in hip Nike campaigns, taken cameos on *Entourage,* sat in Jon Stewart's guest chair, or otherwise resonated with American tastemakers. Inasmuch as Federer or Nadal cares about boosting his profile on the American sportscape, it won't come by winning an event in Madrid or Monte Carlo or Tokyo. The Wimbledon final represents one of their few opportunities to pierce the public consciousness in the United States.

Both Federer and Nadal display what sports shrinks call "excellent body language" on the court. Unlike most other players, they seldom let their movements or their posture or their facial expressions indicate whether they're winning or behind. Tamping down their emotions, they neither sulk much when they're losing nor exult much when they're ahead. But at the start of the second set, Federer wore a mask of exasperation. He'd later admit that he'd played a reasonably good first set and executed his game plan and suppressed his nerves. One sloppy early game had doomed him. But it all gave rise to a larger source of frustration. Against everyone else, Federer can play *his* game—the game he wants to play—and still win. Against Nadal, he can't simply play his style. He has to make adjustments and think differently and face discomfort, all the while knowing the opponent on the other side of the net has never shown an instinct to submit.

Federer walked hurriedly to the baseline to begin the match's second act. Barely pausing between points, wiping his brow on his wristband without requesting a towel, he deployed his moves as if playing tennis's answer to speed chess. It took him exactly one minute to hold serve at love. Nadal slowed the pace on his service game, but he could do little to slow his opponent. Federer had entered the Zone, the blissful and fleeting interval during which an athlete feels infallible. The laws of space and physics are suspended. Time is elastic. The extraordinary becomes ordinary. Almost ruthless in their accuracy, Zoning tennis players feel that they can guide the ball wherever they please. Anything the brain devises, the body can execute. Serves pop off the racket. The opponent's shots travel slowly, and when the ball finally arrives, it appears to be the size of a melon.

While Nadal is an uncommonly stable, steady player who seldom strays from his normal level, Federer is particularly prone to these patches of brilliance. On the first point, Federer, suddenly so free, so unconstrained, unfurled a whimsical drop shot. Nadal was barely able to retrieve the ball and Federer put away an easy volley. On the next point Nadal reverted to the safety of his game plan: hitting every shot to Federer's backhand. Emboldened, Federer blasted away. *Think that's my weak side? How do you like these apples?* When Nadal finally reversed course and directed the ball to the corner, Federer rifled a forehand that nearly left a divot in the grass. Love–30. It was another reminder that, for as often as Federer-Nadal is reduced to brain-versus-brawn, that's really far too simplistic. Nadal is no dummy. And Federer can smack the hell out of the ball.

A minute later, Federer held break point. Nadal attacked the net with an offering that bounced to his opponent's forehand. Federer glided into position and then held his shot, giving no indication where he was about to hit the ball. At the last instant, he rolled his wrist, imparting topspin, and zapped a crosscourt winner. The ball had barely skidded past Nadal when Federer let loose a yell from deep in his diaphragm that sounded like a cross between "Yeaahhhh" and "Jaaaaahh." In his cheering section there were fist-pumps all around.

Still in the Zone, Federer continued to build his lead with another brisk and businesslike game. Acutely aware of his surroundings, Federer was about to serve when he noticed a ball girl had failed to pick up a stray ball. He looked up, urged her to retrieve it, and gently used his racket to direct her to the proper station. This was Federer's stage, and if he could help it, even the extras were going to be in perfect position. Once the girl had scurried off, Federer concluded the game with a service winner. Nadal labored to hold serve, but Federer — no expulsion from the Zone quite yet — rendered his opponent a spectator, again holding serve at love. 4–1. Through just fourteen minutes of play in the second set, Federer had offered a tasting menu of his skills and was two games from leveling the match at a set apiece.

Such displays of sublime tennis lead to the often made observation that Federer plays tennis that is "quintessentially Swiss." A truism in sports: athletes perform in a way that reflects the personality of their home. The Los Angeles Lakers are known for their flair-filled, "Showtime" basketball. The Nebraska Cornhuskers perform with a conservative, incremental approach associated with the American Midwest. Teams from Detroit, Pittsburgh, Buffalo, and other Rust Belt cities are invariably praised for having a "blue-collar work ethic."

This geography-is-destiny phenomenon holds in tennis too. Hailing as they do from the land of SUVs, big-budget action movies, and (at least through 2008) forcefully aggressive foreign policy, American players tend to exhibit a wealth of power and a poverty of nuance. Andy Roddick, James Blake, Venus and Serena Williams, all pulverize the ball. None will ever be described as artistic. Each is the tennis equivalent of a Humvee on the Autobahn. (To subject the analogy to further torture: as the United States' geopolitical and economic supremacy may be waning, the decline is mirrored in tennis. At this writing, it's been more than five years since an American male last won a Grand Slam singles title.) French players, meanwhile, are of-ten stylish and artistic, but, par for a country with shaky re-sults in military conflicts, lack a certain battle-toughness. A top-ranked Gaul, Richard Gasquet, for instance, might pos-sess the most bounteous natural talent this side of Federer, but his lack of ballast — earlier in 2008, he begged off a Davis Cup match not for a specific injury but because he "didn't have self-belief" — has prevented him from fulfilling his boundless po-tential. The Russians often have a sort of clinical power, but, recalling Cold War–era manufacturing, their internal circuitry isn't always right. The famously mercurial Marat Safin is the most obvious illustration.

One takes Federer's "quintessentially Swiss" game to mean that it's precise, centered, measured, organized. Beyond that, it was never made clear to me how he was so representative of the Swiss character. On a slow day at the French Open, I played hooky from the matches and visited Federer's home-town of Basel. A high-speed train left from Paris's Gare de l'Est, whipped through the guts of Alsace-Lorraine, and ar-rived at the Basel station three and a half hours later. The train arrived eight or ten minutes late, which by Amtrak standards would constitute exquisite punctuality. As it was, a Swiss trav-eler hissed that if the conductor knew the train was so far be-hind schedule, he should've had the decency to make an an-nouncement.

This, it turned out, was a fateful day to visit. The city was midway through Art Basel, an art and design exhibition that has developed a worldwide reputation and even spawned a sister event in Miami. Basel was also a few days removed from hosting games in the Euro 2008 soccer championships. This confluence of Euro-chic art lovers and nationalistic soccer fans, competing for hotel rooms and restaurant seats, presented a curious culture clash. Yet despite the milling crowds, Basel felt more like a large village than the small, thriving city of 175,000 that it is.

Basel is wedged between Germany and France, and the borders are essentially irrelevant. The Basel airport is in France; some Basel business offices are in Germany. Federer's parents joke that they can wake up in Switzerland, play golf in Germany, eat lunch in France, and think nothing of it. The place feels far more Teutonic than Gallic—for linguistic reasons, one suspects, as much as anything else—but just as Switzerland defiantly refuses to enter the European Union, preferring to maintain some detachment, Basel has a distinct personality all its own.

Like a calibrated machine, all the gears smoothly synchronized, Basel just seems to *work*. It's conspicuously clean and conspicuously quiet. It's pragmatic—a ferry across the Rhine is propelled not by a motor but by the river's strong current—with an abundance of culture and a paucity of crime. The public transportation is excellent; graceful high-tech streetcars glide down tracks, converge in the center of town, and then head off in all directions. Basel pulls off the shotgun marriage between old and new, tradition and progress. To wit: one cliché-conforming chocolate shop on a cobblestone street offers free wireless Internet access. It's a city flush with millionaires, but you'd never know it. It's a business hub, yet confrontation, slick salesmanship, and aggressive marketing are discouraged.

Founded in 44 B.C. as a settlement by the Romans, Basel

was a longtime center for textiles and dyeing. Eventually all those chemists turned their attention to pharmaceuticals and life sciences. Dozens of high-tech companies based in Basel are in constant search of talented and educated labor, especially engineers. This shift was embodied by Robert Federer (pronounced FAY-der-er), who was born into a family of textile workers in Berneck, a hamlet in eastern Switzerland near the border of Austria and Lichtenstein. After finishing school, Robert moved to Basel and took a job with the pharmaceutical behemoth Ciba.

In his mid-twenties, he grew restless and migrated to South Africa, mostly, he says, because of the ease in getting a visa. He found a job working for a Ciba plant there. The office secretary was an attractive, lively eighteen-year-old brunette, Lynette Durand. The two began a relationship, often playing tennis on their dates. They married in 1973 and moved back to Switzerland. Thickly built with a ready smile and an unimposing manner, Robert made friends easily. He operated on a level emotional plane and rose quickly at Ciba. Lynette found work there too.

The couple had a daughter, Diana, in 1979. Then, in the summer of 1981, Lynette gave birth to a son. They named him Roger and declined to give him a middle name. Armchair linguists have noted that the name Roger derives from the Germanic words for "fame" (*hrod*) and "spear" or "weapon" (*ger*). "Feder" means "feather" in German. The boy, of course, would one day find fame using his spear as a feather.

Sports fans—and the sports media—like it when athletes have a rich history, a backstory, that helps us make sense of their greatness. This boxer grew up in abject squalor, so it's only natural he'd have such well-honed survival instincts. That basketball player was raised by a single mother under heavy financial pressure; no wonder he has the poise to knock down that jump shot. In Federer's case, his upbringing was conventional if not idyllic—an intact family, middle-class comforts, no apparent trauma—and as a result, it tends to get minimized if not altogether dismissed. In his essay "Roger Federer as Religious Experience," the unrivaled late American writer David Foster Wallace (who would kill himself a few months after the 2008 Wimbledon final) wrote: "Anything you want to know about Mr. Roger N.M.I. Federer—his background, his home town of Basel, Switzerland, his parents' sane and unexploitative support of his talent, his junior tennis career, his early problems with fragility and temper, his beloved junior coach . . . his old-school stoicism and mental toughness and good sportsmanship and evident overall decency and thoughtfulness and charitable largesse—it's all just a Google search away. Knock yourself out."

Yet you could just as easily argue that the unremarkable nature of Federer's childhood makes the success that followed all the more remarkable. And all the more worthy of discussion, not dismissal. How did this kid who grew up under pleasant circumstances familiar to millions of others become perhaps the most accomplished tennis player ever to draw breath? Genetics surely don't explain it. A quick scan of Lynette and Robert Federer, both of average height and build at best, and you would not exactly peg them as the progenitors of a singularly skilled athlete. What then?

Federer was born with a gift—the hand-eye coordination, the timing, the instincts, the sports equivalent of a musician's perfect pitch, the Mozart/Beethoven thing. This was apparent early on. The soundtrack of the Federers' tasteful middle-class home in the Basel suburb of Münchenstein was the *ping* of kicked or thrown or smacked balls caroming off the walls and floors. One of the perks of working for a Basel pharmaceutical firm at the time was a family membership in the company-affiliated sports clubs. Roger would follow his parents to the Ciba tennis club. First the adults would play. Then he'd get a turn with a wooden racket. He was four at the time, and damn if he couldn't meet the ball and maneuver it across the net.

When Roger was eight, Lynette deposited her son at T. C. Old Boys, an unassuming club founded in the 1920s, situated in a quiet park a few miles from Basel's city center. The junior tennis program was run by Madeleine Bärlocher, a placid figure, at once stern and maternal, who herself had once played the Wimbledon girls' tournament. ("I couldn't adjust to the grass," she says, wincing at the memory a half century later.) She recalls Lynette Federer bringing her lanky son to the club and, fatefully, saying, "Here is Roger. I think he can already hit many shots. Maybe you can train him."

Instantly, Bärlocher and the club's other junior coach, a Czech native named Seppli Kacovsky, saw that Roger had what she calls "some special things." But then again, a lot of kids did, not least Emmanuel Marmillod, a teenager with a flowing left-handed game who had recently played in an ATP event and was the benchmark against which all the juniors at T. C. Old Boys were measured. If Federer worked hard and everything broke right, maybe one day he could achieve the heights of Marmillod. Maybe he could become a top Swiss player. No one spoke in terms of minting a future pro, much less in terms of a future champion.

To his parents' frustration, Federer was an indifferent, restless student in school, not dim, but not particularly dedicated. Tennis, however, fed something in him and commanded his full attention. Afternoons, he would ride his bike to T. C. Old Boys and take lessons, both privately and in a group setting. He took to instruction but also taught himself, mostly through experimentation. He found that with little difficulty he could mimic the hooking serves of Sampras and the volleys of Edberg. The "trick shots" didn't seem particularly tricky. The spins and angles that eluded even the best older players at the club seemed to come naturally to Federer. So did the one-handed backhand.

The club had hired a handsome and charismatic Australian, Peter Carter, to work with the most talented juniors. He became the classic mentor figure to Federer, the big brother he'd never had. On the club's half-dozen clay courts, Federer would work with Carter, practicing and repracticing his strokes. He had given up other sports, notably soccer, to concentrate on tennis. Gradually he aimed for smaller and smaller targets on the court, giving himself an increasingly slim margin of error. Federer's abundant talent was masked by his disposition. He was "a clown," as Bärlocher puts it. "Roger wasn't misbehaving but he was very social, wanting to be friends with the other boys. He was smiling, laughing, shouting. He wasn't saying, 'I need to be serious because I can be number one someday.' Not at all."

At the same time, the boy was emotionally sensitive in the extreme, known to leak tears at the slightest setback. Bärlocher recalls Federer losing a match against a player from a rival club. When Bärlocher went to console him, he was nowhere to be seen. "Then I see him on Court One," she says. "He was there sitting alone under the umpire's chair, crying."

The arc of a tennis career often begins so early, a highly attentive parent almost seems to be a prerequisite for success. Would Andre Agassi have reached his heights had his father, Mike, not forcefully pushed from the beginning, introducing his three-year-old son as "the future number one tennis player in the world"? Tennis is such an emotionally draining, solitary pursuit that when some players enter their teenage years, they need a parent to sustain their commitment. Martina Hingis's famously intense mother, Melanie Molitor, once suggested that without her guidance and steadying influence, her daughter might "get a boyfriend or decide she enjoys horseback riding more and *pfft* tennis is done." And once players turn professional, they often need strong parents to look out for their interests. A few weeks before the 2008 Wimbledon, while Novak Djokovic was playing in the Hamburg event, his father reportedly barged into a Belgrade radio station simulcasting the match and berated the tennis commentator for not cheering forcefully enough for his son.

Federer gives the lie to all of this. His parents weren't pushy; if anything, they were "pully." If they nudged him at all, it was to stop taking tennis so seriously. As Bärlocher recalls it, Robert Federer, usually hard at work, was seldom around the club. Essentially Swiss, he was sometimes wary of his son's directing so much intensity and energy into one pursuit. When Roger threw tantrums, Robert took a boys-will-be-boys approach. "I wasn't getting so mad at Roger," he says. "He was a good sport, very laid-back with everyone but himself. If a boy gets frustrated and throws his racket to the fence, I don't mind it as long as he's not cheating. That's what I told Roger: cry when you lose, cry when you win. That's sport. Just don't cheat."

Lynette Federer, pointedly not Swiss, was a stronger tennis player than Robert—to this day, she remains a member of T. C. Old Boys—and showed more ambition. But she, too, would never be taken for a Tennis Parent. When her son was on the court, she was usually away from his match, chatting with friends on the patio. When Roger was twelve or so, he won a match against a player from a competing club. "He played so well!" Bärlocher exclaimed to Lynette. "Yes," Lynette said, "but he behaved so badly! I could hear him yelling from here!"

René Stauffer, an excellent Swiss sports journalist, tells this story: When Federer was a young teenager and first starting to earn notice, he was interviewed by a local newspaper and asked what he would buy with his first tennis paycheck. The paper printed Federer's response: "A Mercedes." Lynette was so shocked by her son's crassness and immodesty that she contacted the reporter, a friend, and asked if she could hear the tape of the interview. Sure enough, Federer had given a less audacious answer. What would he buy with his first winnings? "*Mehr CDs,*" he said in Swiss German. More CDs.

Bärlocher recalls just one time when Lynette insinuated herself into Roger's training. After one practice she suggested that her son might benefit from being moved into a group with older, more competitive players. Bärlocher and Peter Carter happily complied. When Roger heard about his "promotion," he complained that he was being separated from his friends. He asked to be moved back.

Maybe herein lies the answer — at least *an* answer — to the mystery of Federer. Instead of supplementing God-given sports talent with burning ambition and intense training, perhaps it needs to be depressurized. Instead of saddling their son with expectations, the Federers stressed fun. Instead of suggesting to their son that he was special, the Federers took the opposite approach, taking pains to treat Roger no differently than their daughter, Diana. Instead of whisking the kid off to a strength coach, a sports psychologist, a nutritionist, or an herbalist after his lessons at the club, they were happy for him stick around, talking about professional wrestling or soccer or heavy-metal music with other kids he considered to be teammates, not opponents. Maybe this relentless onslaught of normal — natural fertilizer, so to speak — is precisely what abnormal talent requires for growth.

Before long, Federer was coming to terms with his potential. In 1995, he won the Swiss national title for fourteen-and-unders. He made the difficult decision to leave the chrysalis of

Basel and train three hours away, at the Swiss National Tennis Center at Ecublens, a French-speaking town near Lausanne and Lake Geneva. In terms of tennis, it was the right move. Competition was getting hard to come by at T. C. Old Boys. Federer had even surpassed the great Marmillod, who suffered some unfortunate injuries and wasn't panning out as a pro. But Federer was miserable at the academy, homesick and lonely. He didn't speak much French at first (though, as if Federer needed another talent, he had a gift for languages and would become nearly fluent within months). He would return home on the weekend and cry on Sunday afternoon when it was time to return to Ecublens. There, he behaved as if he were suffering from low-grade depression, crying openly, sleeping heroically, and showing little interest in anything other than tennis.

With intense coaching and enhanced competition, Federer made steady progress. A fortuitous growth spurt helped out as well. Though Robert Federer looks to be about five foot seven, with a low center of gravity and small sausages for fingers, his son was blessed with an ideal tennis body: sufficiently tall to generate power, but not so tall as to limit movement. His arms grew disproportionately long, giving a reach advantage, especially on returns. He was sinewy strong with deceptively powerful legs and almost elastic flexibility. (Later, he would work like hell to get even stronger, fitter, and more flexible.)

Inasmuch as Federer was built like the perfect tennis specimen, mentally he was a terminal hothead, conforming to the well-worn stereotype of a tennis brat. A missed shot would trigger a Vesuvian eruption. He'd curse and scream and sulk. He'd toss his racket and, on occasion, subject it to the full Pete Townshend smash job. Sven Groeneveld, the former head of the Swiss Tennis Federation and now a well-regarded coach, tells what he calls "the curtain story." In the late 1990s, a set of drapes adorned with sponsor logos was installed behind the indoor court at a new Swiss national training center. Shortly after the curtains were hung, Federer endured a particularly unfulfilling practice and was in a foul mood. He chucked his racket into the curtains with enough force that it shredded the fabric. Groeneveld demanded that Federer pay for the cost of repair and spend several days assisting the custodians. "It wasn't that he was a bad kid at all," says Groeneveld, "but he could just lose it."

Years later, Federer's transformation from churlish to demure and well-mannered, from McEnroe-esque fire to Borgian ice, would become a central part of the Roger narrative. But this essential point is often lost in the retelling: Federer's rage was directed not at coaches or officials or line judges or opponents. It was directed inward. It was his own errors, a failure to live up to his own standards, that set him off. Endowed with this embarrassment of riches, able to unsheathe so many weapons, he couldn't abide anything less than perfection.

Federer quit his schooling at sixteen. There are the occasional slips that expose his abbreviated education — a few years ago, he was asked a question about Sigmund Freud and awkwardly admitted that, no, the name didn't ring a bell. ("Don't know him. Who is he?") Were it not for tennis, his parents suspect he would have gone to college like most Swiss kids of a certain background and sensibility. But dropping out of school to give himself over to tennis was the right career move.

In spite of his temper, Federer was a top international junior player. In 1998, he was invited to play the Wimbledon junior event and was thoroughly awed by the occasion. Hardly displaying an outsized sense of entitlement or ambition, Federer was so nervous and awestruck before his first match that he asked the umpire to measure the net, which to his eyes looked as if it had been set for volleyball. Nope, it's regulation height, he was told. Federer soon gathered himself and won the tournament.

Later that year he played in the Orange Bowl, the big-ticket junior event held in Miami. He was nearly forced to withdraw with a self-induced injury. Stauffer recalls that before the tournament began, Federer was jumping rope while doing a Tarzan-and-Cheetah impersonation. He landed awkwardly on his foot, and it began to swell up. Even with his foot bandaged, Federer won the title, beating Guillermo Coria, a fleet-footed Argentine, in the final. The Orange Bowl title convinced Robert Federer that his son was, if not destined for greatness, at least sufficiently talented to drop out of school and pursue a career as a professional tennis player. "I felt like I could let him go without fear," Robert says. "If he didn't succeed, okay, he didn't succeed. But when he won the juniors it was like, 'Maybe he really is a hell of a talent.'"

The Orange Bowl event also served as a reminder that Federer was still a kid, fine-tuning his identity, prone to making regrettable decisions. At one point during the tournament, Federer was seized by the impulse to dye his hair blond. When he returned home, his parents were livid, particularly when they learned that this ridiculous styling job had cost close to $250. Bärlocher recalls that she held a junior tournament at T. C. Old Boys a few days after the Orange Bowl. Federer arrived wearing a hat pulled low over his head. "I said to him, 'Take your hat off.' He said, 'I can't. My mom is so mad at me!'" she recalls. "Streaking your hair like that? It's funny to us now, but it's not something a Swiss youngster would do."

With little fanfare, Federer turned pro, pegged as an intriguing prospect but hardly a world beater. He had made the excruciating decision to hire as his coach Peter Lundgren, a barrel-chested former Swedish pro, and not his mentor, Peter Carter. Lundgren had worked previously with Marcelo Rios, an obscenely talented, obscenely temperamental Chilean. Lundgren knew something about the challenge of trying to harness unbridled talent.

For all the players—including Nadal—who try to complicate their game, struggling to add components and diversify their portfolio of shots, Federer was always faced with the opposite problem. He needed to simplify. In the pro game it takes roughly one second for a ball to sail across the net and land on the other side of the court. In that time, Federer had to consider an entire battery of options—spin, angle, location, speed. "If you don't have many dimensions to your game, sometimes that's easier," he says. "You do what you do best. I had many selections, and when I made the wrong one, it could be agony."

Early in his pro career, Federer played on a Swiss professional "mini-tour," foraging for all-important ranking points at four Swiss satellite events. The first event was held in Küblis, an Alpine resort town popular with skiers. Federer had already signed with an agent, and thanks to wild card entries —carrots management agencies dangle in order to entice junior players to sign with them—he played in higher-profile ATP events, including a match against Andre Agassi at the Basel Open. Federer wasn't thrilled about chasing ranking points in rinky-dink Swiss backwaters, and he let that be known. In his first match, he grew frustrated and then played as if shot with a tranquilizer gun. The tournament referee approached Lundgren and asked what the hell was going on. "Would you mind if I penalize him?"

"Not at all," said Lundgren. "Maybe *you* can get through to him."

Federer not only lost the match but stood accused of violating a "best effort" rule and was fined roughly $100, exceeding the prize money he had "earned" that week. The punishment, though, had the intended effect. He won the following event and took the overall points title for the Swiss mini-tour.

So it went for the next five years. Federer resembled the tortured genius, alternately offering tantalizing glimpses of his limitless potential and revealing his potential for self-destruction. Lundgren recalls that after lousy practices, he would take Federer for a drive. He'd roll up the windows, crank up the Metallica, and let the kid scream at the top of his lungs, offloading excess emotion. And that was before the tournament had even started. At night, Federer would lie on his bed and smack his head into the pillow — "head-banging" was the term he gave it — until he finally fell asleep. "What a ball of stress," says Lundgren, shaking his head at the memory.

Federer had his first real breakthrough at Wimbledon in 2001 when he knocked out Pete Sampras, the seven-time champion. He played expert serve-and-volley tennis. He moved gracefully. He served forcefully. He essentially out-Samprased Sampras, playing classic grass court tennis. It was hailed as a "changing of the guard."

Then Federer, slowed by a groin injury, lost his next match with a flat effort. A year later, he returned to Wimbledon, tipped by many as a threat to win, but bowed out in the first round. A few weeks later in that summer, he was dealt a further setback. At Federer's urging, Peter Carter traveled with his family to South Africa, a trip planned to celebrate his wife's apparent recovery from Hodgkin's disease. Touring Kruger National Park, Carter was riding with a guide in a Land Rover when it plunged off a bridge and overturned. Carter, then thirty-seven, died instantly. Federer was playing an event in Toronto when he got the news. He bounded out of his hotel room and ran through the streets of a strange city, hot tears streaming down his face. It was, his mother says, the first real trauma Federer had faced in his life, and it would take him months to recover.

As recently as 2003, Federer was embedded in the top 10 but still a maddeningly erratic performer, "stressed-out" (his term) over results that shorted his potential. At that year's French Open, Federer arrived on a hot streak and was touted by many as the favorite. He lost his first match to Luis Horna, a Peruvian journeyman, a defeat that still makes Federer crinkle his face. "You know how people say 'I left it all out there?'" he says. "I walked off the court that day knowing that I had much more left in me." It was such a desultory performance that one rudely sarcastic writer (okay, this rudely sarcastic writer) was driven to write the following "Ode to Federer," intended to be sung to the tune of "If I Only Had a Brain," from *The Wizard of Oz.*

> If you want to win a wager,
> Bet against me in a Major,
> I can barely hold my serve.
>
> I play exquisitely in patches,
> But choke in big-time matches,
> Because I have no nerve.
>
> Too bad I'm not more gallant,
> As I have vast amounts of talent,
> Plus I play with verve.
>
> But there's love (and not much kissing)
> When I'm doing my Swiss missing
> If I only had some nerve.

And after that, the deluge. Just a few weeks after that dismal French Open disappointment, Federer won the 2003 Wimbledon title, his long-awaited breakthrough. Naturally, he dissolved into tears when presented with the trophy. Some

athletes reach the summit and then find themselves wanting
for motivation. *Now that I've reached the top and can die happy,
what's left to achieve?* For Federer, the title had a catalytic effect,
as if a spigot had been tapped. "For me, it was 'I've proved
something to everyone, including, honestly, myself,'" he says.
"Now that the pressure was off, I honestly felt like a different
player . . . No more anxiety on the court, not so easily disap-
pointed." Suddenly all the best byproducts of winning—faith
in one's talent, self-possession, professionalism, an aura—accrued to Federer. The "talented head case" had been transformed into a champion. That first Wimbledon title would
inaugurate the most dominant five-year run in the history of
men's tennis.

Federer's tennis was damn good. But so was his timing.
He came of age when Boris Becker had retired, Pete Sampras
was winding down his gilded career, and the reformed Andre
Agassi was a fan favorite but a waning talent. At the time, the
two best players in their prime, Lleyton Hewitt and Marat
Safin, were short of physical prowess and mental prowess, re-
spectively. There was no obvious incumbent Federer needed
to unseat, no monster that had to be slain before he could be
No. 1.

Intergenerational comparisons in sports are fun but ultimately pointless, filled as they are with so many variables.
Sure, Nadal would have been a peerless champion in the 1950s,
when players' serves traveled so slowly they could have been
clocked with a sundial. But then again, what if, say, Rod Laver
had the benefits of today's fitness training, nutritional science,
and racket and string technology? Laver won the Grand Slam
with a wooden truncheon; imagine what he would have done
with a graphite wand, a monitored diet, and a medical trainer
positioned courtside.

Still, Federer's reign—a dozen Major titles in five years;

eighteen straight Major semifinals; an uninterrupted run at
No. 1; all at a time when tennis has never been more global,
the field never deeper, the players never better conditioned — is
unsurpassed in men's tennis. Unlike Borg and Laver, Federer
won on hard courts. Unlike Sampras, he won on clay. By 2008,
even the other candidates were essentially willing to concede
that, yes, Federer was the Greatest Tennis Player of All Time.

In Switzerland, Federer's success was met with . . . well,
what? Understated enthusiasm? A reserved pride? Certainly
the Swiss have taken a measure of joy and satisfaction in Federer's accomplishments. But they have not exactly lionized him.
When Federer won Wimbledon for the first time, he appeared
on a balcony above Basel's de facto town square, recalling royalty soaking up the adulation of his subjects. Then, when the
ceremony had ended, he came down and everyone left him
alone.

When Federer moved into a modern, Ian Schrager–style
apartment in the hills of the Basel suburb of Oberwil, he was
perceived as just another twentysomething resident. Neighbors
would see him carrying his laundry or picking up juice at the
store. When the Zeus of tennis passed, no one broke stride,
much less dug into a purse for a camera phone. (Inevitable Tiger comparison: at the time, Woods was living in a doge's palace at Isleworth, an ultraexclusive, double-gated community
outside Orlando.)

When he won Wimbledon for the *fifth* time, someone finally scrawled the graffito "King Roger" on a wall near Federer's apartment. Otherwise there was no indication he lived in
town. He could eat in a restaurant without interruption. He
could go for a run in the streets without fear of inciting a riot.
Federer recently left Oberwil and now splits his time between
apartments in the Lake Zurich village of Wollerau and the oil-

rich phantasmagoric emirate of Dubai. But he's similarly unbothered.

In Basel, there is no strain of Federer-mania. No signs bear
his face. No steakhouses or sports bars borrow his name. No
souvenir shops. No signs at the city limits advising travelers
they are entering "Federer Country." In the summer of 2008,
billboards scattered around Basel featured soccer players ad-
vocating a particular brand of yogurt. Catherine Zeta-Jones's
pleasing visage beamed from a store window, encouraging
passersby to change their mobile service provider. On television and in the Basel newspaper, there was abundant coverage of the art show and soccer matches, but scant mention of
Federer, the local boy made *gut*. There are no large-scale monu-
ments to Federer; rather, his face graces a postage stamp. Heinz
Gunthardt, the former Swiss player, now a tennis commentator, has an interesting theory. Switzerland, he notes, never had
a king. And so the notion of hero worship—of placing others
on a higher plane, no matter how impressive their accomplishments—is foreign.

Even at T. C. Old Boys one would scarcely know the place
had played a major role in harvesting the world's top player.
There are no mentions of Federer outside the club or in the
membership brochure. Inside the Old Boys' modest clubhouse, three autographed photos of Federer adorn the back
wall. (Bärlocher says that she would gladly install a fourth if
Federer were ever to win that elusive French Open title.) But
that's about it. It was explained to Bärlocher that, were this
the United States, the club would have been rechristened in
Federer's honor; there would be an admission charge for visitors; the membership brochures would be available on eBay;
the club would be located on Roger Federer Drive, or some
such. Somehow they would capitalize on this link to history.

"That would not be Swiss at all," she said, giggling as she envisioned a lapse into such crassness. "Roger would be so very embarrassed!"

Besides, she says, T. C. Old Boys—where, incidentally, the onetime prodigy Emmanuel Marmillod is now a teaching pro—has renamed one of its courts in Federer's honor. Indeed, hanging on the back wall of a court is a black-and-white sign roughly the size of a license plate that reads, "Roger Federer Court." So there. But it's hard not to notice that a sign on an adjoining windscreen reading *"Sport macht Spass"*—rough translation: *Sports are fun*—is much larger.

Federer has been an uncommonly versatile player, winning in a variety of ways, on every surface, year-round, under all sorts of circumstances. He has won tournaments at a dizzying clip. There's been no off-court melodrama to speak of. Unversed in the ways of American celebrity, Federer has been subject to no nasty divorces, no paternity suits, no drug arrests.

He's been self-sufficient too. In 2004, Federer dumped Lundgren when he outlived his usefulness. It was a surprising firing, but a few years later, Federer shed light on his decision when he said, "I think it's important to have a lot of respect for your coach, because that sometimes can go away. Especially when you make the breakthrough with somebody . . . You're looking up to the coach before, and all of a sudden the coach is looking up to you." Since then, Federer has seldom employed a coach. And for several years, even as a champion with rocketing global popularity, he carried on without an agent. When Federer was still a junior player, he had signed a management contract with IMG, the Cleveland-based marketing giant. In 2002, Federer's agent, Bill Ryan, left IMG under unpleasant circumstances. Federer made the decision to represent himself, with some help from his parents and business-savvy family friends. The management decisions were made over a kitchen table, not in an oak-paneled conference room. The Federers named this alliance the Hippo Company, a nod to the animals the family had seen while vacationing in South Africa.

Though noble, it made lousy business sense. During the period of self-representation, Federer signed a contract with Nike that, sources say, guaranteed only $1 million in annual income. While Federer could—and did—earn much more in performance-based bonuses, it was a laughably low-ball contract for a figure of Federer's magnitude. The deal became the bane of other tennis agents. When they met with Nike to negotiate deals for their players, Nike reps were known to begin meetings by slapping a copy of Federer's contract on the table. *This is Roger Federer's deal. Surely you don't think we're paying your client more than we pay Roger Federer.* (In 2005, Federer returned to IMG and now has a Nike deal purportedly worth more than $10 million a year.) Even today, his entourage is strikingly bare; the usual membrane that protects an athlete from the adoring masses is mercifully thin. Until recently, fans coveting Federer's autograph needed only to visit his website and mail a note to Robert and Lynette at their home address. Within a month, a signed glossy would arrive.

As he kept winning, Federer found a middle ground between modesty and false modesty. "I don't think you have to be cocky, but sometimes you can be self-confident about what you are achieving," he says. "I also don't think it's the right way to go about things to say 'Oh, it's such a surprise' every time, and 'I can't believe I did it again,' because I come here to win these things, and when I do it's a great satisfaction. I think you have to be honest about things."

Another extraordinary aspect of Federer's reign: his relationships with his colleagues. Inasmuch as Federer is a monarch, he rules with what political science types call "Soft Power." He influences not with militarism or an overweening manner but with culture and ideology and moral authority. The teenager who perceived his opponents as teammates brought the same sensibility to bear when he became the world's top-ranked player. In his mind, he was playing less against the guy on the other side of the net than against the ball and the possibilities presented.

Historically, the top tennis stars have operated at a remove, akin to the popular kids in high school who don't mingle with the members of the Model Boat Society and Audio-Visual Club. Pete Sampras, the Williams sisters, Maria Sharapova . . . part of their aura derives from projecting a sense that they inhabit rarefied air, that they're too good for the tennis commoners. The American doubles star Mike Bryan recalls entering an event headlined by Andre Agassi yet never seeing him the entire week. "Andre never showed up at the practice courts or the locker room. He showed up for the match and got out, took his helicopter or whatever."

Federer takes the opposite approach. He is everywhere. He's not the nose-in-the-air prom queen; he's the student council president. Earlier in his reign, Federer was the popular prankster who would sing in the locker room showers and, when asked to pipe down, emerge to do full Pavarotti histrionics. (Imagine for a moment Tiger Woods, even a young Tiger Woods, standing naked in the locker room and robustly singing.) For a while, the voice mail message on his cell phone was "Hello." The caller, thinking Federer had answered, would begin speaking. "Hey, Roger, what's up?" Then the rest of the message would kick in. "Gotcha, didn't I? Leave me a message." He would run the card games in the players' lounge and invite officials to share rides in the courtesy cars the tournament provided him.

As his sphere of influence grew (and as he matured), Federer found different ways to make everyone in his orbit feel comfortable. He engaged himself in hopelessly snarled tennis politics, serving on the ATP Player Council, and happily became a figurehead for tennis charities. He knows even the most obscure doubles players by name. Recently he taped a message for a media training orientation video for up-and-coming junior players, demystifying the interview process. At the end, Federer stares into the camera and says, unscripted: "I wish you good luck. I'll see you on tour, and you know what? When you come on tour, if you see [me], don't hesitate to ask questions. Me, I'm always happy to talk to you guys and help you . . . anything you want to ask me, don't hesitate, don't be shy. See you around, and all the best."

By accident or design—he insists it's the former—Federer has created a sort of Stockholm syndrome. That is, he triggers a perverse affection among the players he torments. Genuinely fond of Federer, the rest of the field often seems unable to summon much competitive juice when on the other side of the net. He is less a player than he is a phenomenon. A striking example: on the social network site Facebook, there's a group devoted to Federer called "If tennis were a religion then Federer would be God." One of the "officers" responsible for setting up and monitoring the group is John Isner, an American pro whom Federer once played (and, naturally, beat) in the third round of the 2007 U.S. Open.

"It's amazing," says Mats Wilander. "Ninety-five guys out of the top hundred fear him—you can practically smell it when you walk in the locker room—but they also like him." As James Blake says: "He seems like one of the guys in the locker room. Then you go out there, he beats the crap out of you, you come back in the locker room, and he's one of the guys. I mean, it's not intimidation by him being extremely huge or muscular, talking down to anybody, being condescending, having any sort of a huge entourage, keeping him isolated. He's just that good." Andy Roddick's famous quote to Federer perhaps sums it up best: "I'd love to hate you, but you're really nice."

Some cynics will suggest that this odd dynamic—an unwritten noncompete clause, as it were—is all a calculated, keep-your-enemies-closer tactic, that Federer has cleverly tenderized the opposition by being so sociable. But really it's just Federer's nature, his default mode. Whether it's hanging his warm-up jacket neatly on the back of his courtside chair or operating on friendly terms with his colleagues, he'll pick order over chaos every time.

If Federer's disarming humility and dislike of confrontation tends to endear him to the guy on the other side of the net, this nice-guyness can also dull his aura of invincibility. Federer can, and will, win matches simply by outclassing his opponent. But there's also a prevailing sense that if an opponent can pressure Federer, disrupt his cadence and challenge his natural authority, he gives himself a real chance to win.

Toni Nadal counts himself among the Federer-philes. Toni says that when assessing Rafael's game, he doesn't bother trying to incorporate and simulate components of Federer's game because "Roger is too good." When a reporter challenged this assertion—how can you concede that Federer is too good when your player routinely beats him?—Toni clarified: "There is a difference between 'who is better' and 'who knows more.' Better now is Rafael [according to] the ranking. But who has the best game? Federer." Then, in another breath, Toni explains how he reconciles this reverence with a belief that Federer can be beaten: "Roger is an amazing tennis player. But he is human. You put doubt in his head and . . ."

And this is precisely what Toni's nephew began to do in

the second set of the Wimbledon final. With the sun making a cameo appearance, dappling and throwing shadows on the court, Nadal served, trailing 1–4. He not only held his serve but, more important, he managed to evict Federer from the Zone. Federer was suddenly on the defensive, no longer placing shots as if he had sent the ball to obedience school. Forehands sailed; a backhand went wayward and descended into the bottom of the net. Federer has often castigated the drop shot as "a bailout shot," beneath his dignity. Yet he attempted one at this juncture. It was an ill-disguised dink that led to a Nadal smash.

Serving at 4–2, Federer failed to self-correct. At 15–15, Nadal hit a short ball; Federer anticipated and drilled his approach to the corner. On the dead run, Nadal caught up to the ball and then unleashed a forehand that burned through the air. It was a sensational shot that didn't just win the point but had a dispiriting what-do-I-have-to-do-to-beat-this-guy? effect on Federer.

After inducing another error, Nadal suddenly held a break point. Federer slapped a short ball deep to Nadal's backhand. Grunting as he struck the ball, Nadal pasted a backhand up the line. Stationed at the net, Federer lunged for the volley, but the ball sailed off his racket well beyond the baseline. Staring down at the grass, Federer walked to his chair. He had thoroughly outplayed Nadal in the set. And they were back on serve. 3–4.

Nadal sat in his chair, sipping Evian from a bottle and then placing the bottle down, the label sticking out. Even in the throes of the Wimbledon final, he was true to his obsessions. He'd wiggled his conspicuously small feet into conspicuously small white Nikes—European size 42, American size 9½—that he wears extra-tight, "the way a [soccer] player does." He dabbed himself with one of the five thousand official Wimbledon towels provided to the players. (In keeping with a long-standing tradition of players accumulating souvenirs from all four Major tournaments, half of the towels go missing—"I wouldn't say stolen," a Wimbledon spokesperson asserted to a London newspaper, "just not returned.") Without unfixing his gaze from the court, Nadal began his service game.

Serving at 30–0, Nadal guided the ball, of course, to Federer's backhand. By now cheating to that side of the court, Federer struck a clean return. The next dozen shots composed as fine a tennis point as one ever could hope to see, a banquet of power, guile, creativity, athleticism, and improvisation. Federer scythed a sharply angled backhand. Nadal scrambled near the umpire's chair to retrieve the ball. He arrived in time to pound a comparably angled ball that sent Federer sprawling. Showing off his rubber-band flexibility, Federer lunged for a backhand that miraculously landed a few inches inside the baseline. Though it was midpoint, the crowd shrieked. Nadal scrambled after the ball, *overran it,* and yet recovered to slap a spinning, angled forehand back over the net. Surprised, Federer short-hopped a backhand—a difficult shot that he, typically, made look routine—and the rally resumed. It was now rock-concert loud in the stands. Finally, on the fifteenth stroke of the rally, Nadal netted a lazy drop shot.

The fans, many of them standing, applauded like crazy. The television commentators threw out breathless phrases like "simply sensational." Even the staid linesmen shook their heads and tried to stifle smiles after the rollicking point they'd just witnessed. Only two figures in the entire stadium failed to react. Blank expressions on their faces, Federer and Nadal simply retreated to play the next point. It was too crucial a time in the match to emote one way or the other.

At 30–30 Nadal hit an ace that Federer challenged unsuccessfully, again more as a means of relieving anger than because he thought the line call was genuinely incorrect. Federer then fought back to hold a break point, which Nadal saved with a strong serve. For Federer, it was yet another opportunity missed. He controlled the next point and worked his way into a winning position. Nadal floated a desperation lob that Federer prepared to take out of the air, shoulder-high, and crush with a swinging forehand. It's a shot that the teaching pro at your local club probably makes four out of five times, and Federer makes ninety-nine times out of a hundred. But this time, as Federer took his backswing, a fan yelled out, "Come on, Roger!" Distracted, Federer overhit the ball and it sailed beyond the baseline. Over the shocked "ooohs" of the crowd, Federer glowered in the general direction of the voice, contorted his face, and yelled, "Shut up!"

Federer's distracted error and the subsequent outburst were so out of character—hell, even the annoying parents of Novak Djokovic only rated a benign "Be quiet!" a few weeks back —and so un-Swiss that the crowd giggled awkwardly. But here again, Federer was showing his essential humanity. The circumstances were incredibly stressful and filled with passionate energy. And by momentarily snapping, Federer was reacting the way most of us would. Nadal won the game with still another serve to Federer's backhand, this one spinning into the body, a shrewd tactical play. 4–4.

Around this time, Pascal Maria, the chair umpire, noticed something odd. Both players were making eye contact with him, briefly but unmistakably, after almost every point. Even from yards away, even with a box of supporters they could have locked eyes with instead, they seemed to want to make a connection with *him*, the third man on the court. He interpreted it not as a plea for preferential treatment but as a tacit message. "It was like they were saying, 'We need each other's support,' "

Maria would say a few weeks later. "'There will be a winner and a loser, but let's deal with everything together to make it special.'" Though intensely focused on the task at hand, athletes—be they boxers, golfers, or basketball players—usually have the wherewithal to sense when they're part of a truly exceptional sporting event. Federer and Nadal had now reached this point.

As Federer prepared to serve, Nadal rocked slightly, hunched his back, and wrapped his hand around his racket. Besides using an extreme western grip, Nadal also rests a sizable chunk of his meaty hand under the handle of the racket in a way that recalls a caveman clasping a cudgel. When he strikes the ball, instead of using his forward momentum to step into it, he often leans backward and then follows through not by dragging the racket across his body (as Federer does) but by whipping the racket behind his head. Experts and teaching pros readily debate whether Nadal's game is evolutionary or a one-of-a-kind freak phenomenon.

Because of his extreme grip, his whipping follow-through, and his polyester strings (more on this later), Nadal generates unholy amounts of topspin, which brings the ball down without compromising power. Nadal's shots sometimes appeared destined to hit the Royal Box on the fly before, as if suddenly thinking better of the idea, dipping into the court. John Yandell, a California tennis guru, quantified Nadal's uniqueness. Using video capture technology, Yandell determined that Nadal's forehand rotates as fast as 5,000 rpm, twenty percent more spin, on average, than Federer's. When you eyeball their shots, that difference appears to be conservative.

Now Nadal's cutting, gyrating, sidewinding shots caused Federer particular difficulty, as did the wind, which was picking up. Planted behind the baseline, Federer played a tentative service game. He made two unforced errors, then watched

as two of Nadal's spin-laden forehands strafed past him. Incapable of missing just fifteen or so minutes earlier, Federer was
now lapsing in concentration and trailing in the set, 4–5.

Most athletes tend to view the media as a necessary evil, a vital conduit for connecting the consumer with the product, but
also a collective annoyance, an underdressed, overdandruffed
legion of cynics, gossips, and second-guessers. Federer — bless-
edly, from this self-interested perspective — is a shining anom-
aly. For a pro athlete, never mind one of his stature, he is exceptionally accessible and media-friendly. He considers "the
media drill" an attendant responsibility of being the sport's
most prominent figure. This story still makes the rounds in
the pressroom: Several years ago, Federer had finished a match
at the ATP's year-end Masters Cup and was undergoing his
usual regimen of interviews. He was conducting a session
with a Swiss radio journalist when, toward the end, he looked
down to see that the recording device had somehow jammed.
"I think we'd better do the interview again," he said. It was
1:30 in the morning, and he was scheduled to play a match the
next day.

The first year that Federer won the Australian Open, he
spent nearly four hours after the final conducting interviews in
four tongues. Federer once asked Tiger Woods about his media commitment, and Woods responded that even after winning the biggest events, he never spent more than thirty minutes giving interviews.

Surely Federer has done at least an informal cost-benefit
analysis. Those one-on-one interviews, television spots, and
magazine sit-downs have greased the commercial skids, generating all sorts of free publicity for the sport, the tournaments
that often pay him a mid-six-figure appearance fee, the sponsors, the tour, and, of course, for Federer, Inc. Lord knows how

many millions Pete Sampras cost himself by being opaque and detached. Afforded so little of his time, the media naturally characterized Sampras as "boring," the most damning insult in the marketing lexicon.

But for Federer, engaging the media is, if not outright fun, then hardly a big deal. Lynette Federer herself used to volunteer at the media desk of the Basel ATP event, laminating press badges for the same journalists who would soon be seeking interviews with her son. Chatting pleasantly and discussing tennis with a bunch of middle-aged men and women, Federer is thoroughly in his element.

Though perfectly cordial with the media, Nadal is unmistakably less comfortable in the hot seat. Even in Spanish, his answers are guarded and famously bland. He often gently challenges the premise of the question before furnishing a response.

> Q: How did you contend with the heat?
> A: It wasn't so hot, no?

A Nadal operative explains that Rafael is still cautious with his English and prefers to communicate on his blog. Spanish journalists have another take: Nadal didn't grow up in a media-obsessed culture that thrusts the private lives of celebrities into the public domain. There is no Majorcan equivalent of the confessional prime-time interview or *MTV Cribs*. If Nadal is willing to revisit the match he just played, he has neither the interest nor the inclination to voice his opinions or open his soul.

In most sports, at least in the United States, the media policy is fairly simple. The locker room is open for a period of time before the game. Reporters are free to enter and approach athletes with questions. Athletes are free to decline comment — or seek refuge on the training table or in the shower or toilet stall, as is sometimes the case. After the game ends, the media are invited back, usually firing off questions as the athletes get dressed. Tennis is different. Locker rooms are closed to the media; instead, under threat of fine, players must attend post-match press conferences. These sessions can take on the dimensions of a Beckett play. Some questions are truly thoughtful. Some are truly inane. Same goes for the answers. As the player speaks, a stenographer pecks madly on a machine, magically compiling a transcript that awaits the journalists by the time they're back at their pressroom desks.

Federer has mastered this strange, unnatural exercise. Often —though less often in recent years—he disarms the crowd of interrogators with jokes. Then he offers enough thoughtful and fresh sound bites to "feed the beast" while deftly sidestepping tendentious topics. And after conducting the drill in English, he repeats it in German, French, and Swiss German. He once told me that he sometimes gives different answers to the same questions, depending on the language. Just to mess with us? "No, not at all," he said. "I think differently in different languages. It's strange. The way you express yourself—even something like putting verbs at the end of a sentence—it affects how you think."

In his mandatory press conference preceding the Wimbledon final, Federer had been asked about Nadal's tendency to play at a grindingly slow pace and take longer than the allotted twenty seconds between points, particularly when the match tightens. It was a loaded question, designed to roil. Usually Federer bats these back, glibly but evasively. This time he had a pointed response. He sighed, his face barely visible under a baseball cap pulled down to his eyes. "You know, I mean, it's obviously a fine line, you know, because I think until he gets into position to serve, you know, he takes his twenty seconds, whatever, and then he takes another, you know, ten, fifteen seconds until he really serves. It's a tricky situation, you know. But the unfortunate part, let's say, is the umpire will always give him a warning, but he will never give him a point penalty. I'm not saying he abuses it, but he never really feels the heat that much."

Then, like a polished politician, once he got in his shots, he pulled back. "I think he's speeded it up actually a little bit since those times," Federer added. "I actually felt like he was playing fair, you know, lately. He does still play slow, but not as slow as maybe eight matches ago when I played him. Look, it's up to the umpire. I try to concentrate. I don't think I win or lose a match because he takes five seconds extra per point. That's not going to kill me." Translation: True, I've noticed my opponent's dodgy ethics. But I don't want to make a big deal about it. I'll let the voters decide.

Psychological warfare has always ridden in tandem with competition. After all, what Bible story or classical myth doesn't involve an element of psych-out? Boxing has its pre-fight stare-down, baseball its chin-music pitches, basketball its trash talk. All exist for the purpose of mental leverage. And yet it was hard to recall Federer ever indulging in these tactics. He was going to beat you strictly by dint of sheer talent. He was too proud for glowering looks or gamesmanship or provocative remarks. There he was, though, before the Wimbledon final, with a transparent bit of psychological jousting. This was cheered by some. *Finally, Federer engaging in some street fighting.* For others, this departure from standard operating procedure was another sign that Federer was feeling threatened by his rival.

Whatever, Federer's gambit appeared to have worked. Serving at 5–4, 30–30, two points from the set, Nadal stood at the baseline bouncing, bouncing, bouncing the ball. Federer rocked back and forth, flicking his hair and shaking his head slightly as if to say, *While we're still young, pal. Hit the friggin' serve already!* Technically, the permitted twenty seconds between points begins when the ball from the previous point is out of play. But umpires often permit five extra seconds of leeway. Having activated a clock on his electronic scoring pad, Pascal Maria was able to determine that more than thirty seconds had elapsed since the previous point had ended. Still, it's hard to believe that Federer's remarks the previous day hadn't had at least a subconscious effect. As Nadal appeared to begin his motion, Maria spoke: "Time violation. Warning, Mister Nadal."

Yes, Nadal had clearly violated the letter of the law. But there is also an unspoken rule in sports that in the most important intervals, the referees "swallow the whistle." In the waning moments of NBA games, refs will refrain from calling a foul on anything short of physical dismemberment. Same in hockey. Here, at 5–4 in the second set of the Wimbledon final, Maria had insinuated himself into the match. He knew that it was a hell of a time to call an infraction. But the rules are the rules.

In the players' box, Nadal's agent, Carlos Costa, started to rise angrily. Lesser players would have reflexively started berating the chair umpire. Refusing to be extracted from his ectoplasm of calm, Nadal didn't react in the slightest. He paused without looking up, wiped his brow, bounced the ball nine times—thirteen seconds—and served again. Fault long. He tried again, performing a nimble feat of bouncing the ball on his racket with his left hand and knicker-spelunking with the right. He spun his second ball cautiously into the box. Federer again went on the attack, driving a forehand deep into Nadal's backhand corner.

As Federer made a dash toward the net, Nadal took a few short steps and, positioned a yard behind the doubles alley, caught up to the ball. He unfurled a perfect grass court slice shot, cutting the ball at an impossibly short angle. Barely missing the net, the ball landed well within the service line but well out of Federer's reach. Nadal would later recollect that it might have been the best grass court shot he'd ever hit. The crowd erupted. In the box, Costa and Uncle Toni rose together, applauding not just this exquisite piece of shotmaking but their player's ability to ignore distraction and resume the business at hand. Nadal's expression still unchanged, he returned to the baseline, a point from winning the second set.

Federer responded, though, subtly pushing Nadal deeper and deeper in the court until he induced an error. At deuce, Federer flung a wind-aided backhand that appeared to hit a dead patch of grass. Nadal tried to block the ball back but jerked awkwardly and pushed the shot wide. Break point Federer, another big point. Counter to the natural impulse to play conservative tennis at such a precarious interval, Nadal swung uninhibitedly through the next point. He had abbreviated his cyclonic backswing for grass and, contrary to most topspin lovers, his left arm was virtually straight at the point of contact. Grunting with every stroke, he finally blasted a forehand that Federer shoveled into the net.

Emboldened, Nadal whacked a serve that kicked with spin. Resembling a man riding a mechanical bull, Federer jerked erratically to the ball. He blocked it long. Set point. Nadal exhaled, knicker-picked, spun in a serve, and played to Federer's backhand. On the second shot of the rally, Federer seemed to debate whether to hit a slice or a one-handed drive. He was a teenager again, lost among so many damn options. The hesitation was fatal. The infinitesimally small hitch ruined the mechanics. Federer drove the ball into the net. 6–4.

Like those whack-a-moles at the arcade, the entire Nadal contingent popped up in unison. Nadal walked to his chair, emotionless. He had just won five straight games. He had now won the last six sets he had played against Federer. He was one set from winning Wimbledon for the first time.

Third Set

6-7

ON SATURDAY, JULY 5, "Miss Venus Williams," as she is called at the All England Club, defeated her sister, "Miss Serena Williams," to win the Wimbledon ladies' singles title for the fifth time. Now, a day later and a mile or so from the All England Club, Venus sat in the rental apartment—"flat," she trained herself to call it—she and Serena had shared during the tournament. Serena had already packed her bags and caught a flight home, still smarting from defeat in the final, but Venus had stayed in town in order to attend the Wimbledon Champions Ball. Before leaving for England, Venus had packed a formal gown; such was her level of certitude that she would win the tournament.

Held at the Intercontinental Hotel, not far from Buckingham Palace, following the men's final on Sunday night, the Champions Ball is another of those touches that elevate and distinguish Wimbledon from the other Major championships. But it can be hell on the women's winner, who has to sit idly until her male counterpart is determined. When Venus won the women's title for the first time in 2000, she waited around all day Sunday until, in near darkness, Pete Sampras emerged as the men's winner. By the time that match had ended and

Sampras, having fulfilled his media obligations, arrived at the ball, it was well after midnight. Clearly less than thrilled to be attending, Sampras came dressed in a sweatsuit before a club member volunteered his sport coat.

Now, sitting on a couch in her flat, Venus figured that she was going to catch a break this year. Neglecting her packing, she'd become engrossed in watching Federer-Nadal on television. With Nadal having won the first two sets, Venus thought it was about time to change into her gown, taking care of some cosmetic touches, and get on her way. At the rate things were going, the Champions Ball would be just a few hours away.

Between sets, Federer had a brief conversation with himself, not about the two sets he had lost, and not about the implications of losing Wimbledon for the first time since 2002. He spent the changeover monologuing to himself about what he needed to do *now* to alter the course of the match. Federer is risk-averse by nature. (Asked about the 2008 global financial meltdown, Federer said, "I have a big mattress," a comment made in jest, but telling nonetheless.) But for all his conservatism, he realized that to have any chance of reversing the match, he needed to play with less inhibition, especially on the critical points. One of the broadcast networks noted this statistic: There had been ten break points in the match. Nadal had won eight of them. On all other points, Federer was leading 61–58.

Whether it was out of loyalty, pity, or a desire to gorge themselves on more of this high-level, high-drama tennis, the fans roared for Federer between sets. The competing cheers of "Come on, Rajah" outdecibeled "Come on, Rafa" by a considerable margin. His hair tousled by the wind and poking out of his headband, Federer served to begin the third set and instantly conjured his most authoritative tennis. The game spanned just four points, but it was a master class in grass court play. Federer served to the corners and attacked the net and moved—glided, really—seamlessly around the court. Had you just walked into the stadium, you would probably have thought that Federer was cruising, on his inexorable way to another title.

Federer's mix of stylish classicism and flash can be traced to his mechanics. He hits his trademark shot, his forehand, with an open stance and a fairly standard "semi-eastern" grip, essentially shaking hands with the racket, positioning his right hand parallel to the strings. He then splays his right index finger half an inch or so from his other four fingers, shifting it slightly downward. In stark contrast to Nadal's, this is a traditional, conservative grip that enables Federer to generate unholy amounts of pace and power. It also enables him to "play up" and position himself inside the baseline to dictate play— the handshake grip is ideal for hitting the ball when it bounces between the waist and chest. Players using this grip, however, are vulnerable to high-bouncing balls, which they're forced to hit at ear level. So it's to an opponent's benefit to push Federer a yard or two behind the baseline and force him to make contact at shoulder and neck level. Much easier said than done, of course. Unless you're Nadal.

Just as Eskimos have nineteen different words for snow, Federer hits multiple cognates of the forehand. John Yandell, the innovative San Francisco tennis researcher, has studied hours of video and determined that Federer hits *twenty-seven* distinct variations of his forehand, an astoundingly large repertoire. In most cases, Federer assumes an open stance, rotates his hips, and extends his arm in front of his body, all the while betraying the peculiar habit of staring at the racket even after the ball's been struck, appearing to admire his handiwork. But he can also execute the stroke with, say, his back foot elevated off the ground or by using more of his wrist.

Where does Federer get this ability to leaven his power with spin? When he strikes the ball, he rotates his hand and finishes his stroke over his left breast, rather than his left shoulder. This classic "wiper finish," as teaching pros call it, helps generate the kick. When you take into account the melding of the classic grip and the flourishy follow-through, the variations, all the component body parts resembling a sleek machine and working in perfect harmony—the Federer forehand is really the perfect tennis stroke. And it's instructive to recreational players. The average club hacker uses a conservative handshake grip that approximates Federer's. And the twisting of the hand to hit over the ball and end up with a wiper finish isn't a particularly difficult maneuver. As Yandell puts it: "Federer's forehand is both a stroke of genius and, in many ways, a stroke for the masses." Which is to say that, not unlike Wimbledon itself, Federer's game is at once magisterial and populist.

Still grooving his forehand, Federer made Nadal labor to hold serve. 1–1. And then the match nearly ended.

Early in his fourth-round encounter with Mikhail Youzhny, Nadal slipped while chasing a ball. As his body jerked in one direction, his right knee had other ideas. Nadal lay supine on the grass, and the odds of Federer's winning the title suddenly spiked. A television replay of Nadal's slip was uncomfortable to watch. Scared after having heard what he describes as "a little crack from behind," Nadal had summoned Michael Novotny, a multilingual trainer employed during the year by the ATP who, for the sake of continuity and consistency, had been subcontracted by Wimbledon for the two weeks. At the ensuing changeover, Novotny stretched out Nadal's leg, applied an ointment, and bandaged the knee. Between the original assessment and the injury time-out, the treatment lasted nearly nine minutes. Aided by adrenaline, Nadal surrendered just a few more games, polishing off Youzhny in straight sets. But the sensation in his knee was sufficiently intense that Nadal would require painkillers after the match.

For his next two matches, Nadal showed no trace of injury, his mobility not reduced in the slightest. But as a precaution, for the final Novotny stationed himself courtside, behind netting near the players' entrance. For two sets, he stood idly enjoying the match, a spectator with a prime spot. But early in the third set, Novotny's viewing pleasure was interrupted. Serving at 1–1, Federer maneuvered Nadal around the court with a series of penetrating shots. Pouncing on a short ball, Federer pegged a forehand to the left side of the court. Nadal had anticipated a shot to the right. It was a classic case of wrong-footing. As Nadal attempted to self-correct and retrieve the shot, his right knee remained in place like a stubborn child. He fell to the ground, winced, and, in pin-drop quiet, attempted to rise. He fell flat on his back. His ass, already grass-stained, appeared to be plastered to the court. In Nadal's section of the players' box, the faces looked cadaverous. His shirt billowing in the wind, Federer walked to the net, cast a look of concern, and asked Nadal if he was okay. Nadal nodded unconvincingly.

If one critique can be leveled at Nadal's game, it would be that his unceasingly physical, almost violent style of play—all that twisting and pounding and grinding—puts so much stress on his body that he's a medical disaster waiting to happen. One tennis trainer notes that Nadal's Nike court shoes are often uncommonly scuffed and worn by the end of a match. "Why would you think his body would be any different?" Eben Harrell, a fine writer for *Time* magazine, recently asked Rafael Maymo, Nadal's baby-faced physiotherapist, which of Nadal's body parts are under the most strain when he plays. "Shoulder, feet, legs, and back," Maymo responded. Then: "Oh, wait, that's every part." In his brief career, Nadal has already suffered a number of maladies, including an elbow injury, a stress fracture to his left ankle, a foot injury, each of which he initially feared might forestall his career. Now this. At the worst conceivable time.

Anguished, Nadal finally rose and walked gingerly to his chair, ostensibly to change rackets but really to buy some time and collect himself. Passing the chair umpire, Nadal said firmly in his accented English, "Can you call the trainer for the next changeover?" Then he walked back to return serve, wearing a brave face, but he'd later admit to being more than a little scared. "If I cannot move, the match is over, no?" Yes. Were this boxing, Nadal, leading as he was on the judges' cards, could have clutched and grabbed for the rest of the fight. Were this golf, he could have "laid up" and preserved victory by playing conservatively. In basketball, football, or soccer, he could have sustained his lead by running out the clock. But in tennis, time is apportioned by points, not by minutes and seconds. It's simple: the player who fails to win the final point fails to win the match. No matter how well he might have played previously.

Inasmuch as Nadal was in agony, it was no fun for Federer either. Psychologically, it's no picnic playing a wounded opponent. Run him around the court and it feels sadistic, the victory hollow. Take pity on him and you risk losing the match. On the ensuing point, Federer served tentatively—those damn humane impulses—and Nadal won the point with a screaming crosscourt backhand. But this shot, while bolstering Nadal, also had the effect of relaxing Federer. His opponent was no wounded animal, after all. Federer reared back and belted two unreturnable serves to win the game.

At the change of ends, Novotny, the trainer, trotted onto the grass and began ministering to Nadal, poking and prodding and rubbing around his knee. "Put a little cream on it," Nadal said softly in Spanish. Novotny dutifully obeyed. Federer stared ahead and then down at his feet, undistracted by the activity on the other side of the umpire's chair. "It's fine," Nadal then said. "I didn't want to run on it, but it's fine."*

Fortunately this injury, if not a false alarm, looked worse on a television replay than it actually was. Assessing the damage, Novotny determined that Nadal required no time-out. Nadal agreed. Helped by a surge of adrenaline, the pain subsided. All of that prematch stretching and preventive work with Rafael Maymo may have saved Nadal the match. The sense of relief was shared by Federer, who wanted to *beat* Nadal, not just win Wimbledon — especially down two sets to none — by virtue of an injury retirement. When Nadal popped up from his chair and jogged to his side of the court to serve, fifteen thousand fans exhaled in unison.

After that drama, the match resumed its pulse. Federer quickly earned two break points. Nadal eliminated one with a line-licking forehand. On the second, Nadal stopped play midway through the point to challenge a line call on the baseline, believing a Federer shot that had gone uncalled had, in fact, landed out. Because Nadal had stopped play, had he been

---

* The injury triggered several immediate consequences. On-line betting odds lurched in Federer's favor. Also, lured by a sizable guaranteed appearance fee, Nadal had committed himself to play a clay court event in Stuttgart that began the following day. As Nadal writhed on the grass in pain, it was clear that the chances of his playing the following week in Stuttgart were swiftly approaching zero. In New York, an opportunistic orthopedist at the Mount Sinai School of Medicine summoned his publicist to issue an e-mail to a raft of journalists. A "top Sinai expert" was willing to share his thoughts with the media. "Nadal's injury probably came from him working his knee too hard . . . The body is like a rope tying a boat to a dock: it can be gently tugged on and snap back into shape; when a storm comes, it puts excess strain on the rope and the rope frays. Same thing happens to the knee." Never mind that this physician, so generous with his time and expertise, had never treated Nadal, nor was he present at Wimbledon.

wrong he would have lost the point outright. After a tense few seconds, Hawk-Eye determined that the ball had sailed beyond the baseline by less than an inch, a sliver of geography no wider than the distance between here   and here.

Such are the minute differences on which entire matches can turn. In the players' box, Toni Nadal shook his head and marveled at his nephew's eyes. Or his balls.

Two games later, Federer had another chance to insinuate himself into the match. Serving at 15–30, Nadal sliced a backhand wide. The crowd murmured only slightly, but Nadal and Federer, sensing a significance no one else did, reacted with more emotion than either had shown all afternoon. Nadal swatted his racket in frustration, thwacking air molecules. Simultaneously, Federer yelled, "C'mon!"

Again Federer had a pair of break points. Again Nadal prevailed. Federer tightly batted two second-serve returns outside the court, causing his girlfriend, Mirka Vavrinec, to bellow, "Move your feet, Roger!" It all laid bare the abiding irony. This was a match of unimpeachable quality, a festival of breathtaking shots and unrivaled athleticism. But at its core it was still a mental battle. Confirming this thesis, on the subsequent point—a deuce imbued with much less pressure—Federer calmly pasted a forehand winner. On the taut break point, Nadal reeled off an inspired passing shot. On the pressure-free deuce point, Federer coolly stroked a forehand winner. And so it went. "It's brilliant, isn't it?" Tim Henman, the former British player, said in the BBC commentary booth. "They play the point in the deuce box and it looks so easy for Federer. Play the point from the ad box and it's a totally different story." Here, at the moment the great champions are supposed to elevate, Federer appeared to be retreating.

Nadal salvaged the *fourth* break point of the game with a backhand that skidded off the baseline, setting off a small explosion of chalk. Federer issued a pro forma challenge but was already rolling his eyes, conversing angrily with himself, and grimacing in disgust before the ball was confirmed to be "good." When Nadal closed out the game, Toni Nadal tipped his white baseball cap. "You can talk about Rafael's tennis, his forehand, his speed on the court," Toni would later say. "But his mental strength, his playing well when he has to battle, to me that is most important. That's just his character."

The Nadal narrative is set almost exclusively on Majorca (or Mallorca, in Catalan), the largest Spanish island that luxuriates in the Mediterranean, due south of Barcelona and due east of Valencia. For centuries, Majorca was a sort of geographic vanity prize, not essential for military purposes or trade, but a plum piece of land coveted by various empires. The island's history is filled with references to invasions and occupations, sacking and annexing, of Vandals and Byzantines and Moors.

All this upheaval and strife imbued the citizenry with a quiet toughness, but also a so-it-goes ("*qué más dá*") mentality that veers closer to tranquility than to fatalism. A Majorcan epigram translates roughly as: "The world follows its way. Don't worry, don't interfere, just relax and enjoy . . . And then one day you die." Majorcans are proudly Spanish, but, much like their dialect, their character isn't fully understood in Spain, even by other Catalonians. As Nadal puts it, "I think maybe you have to be from Majorca to understand Majorca."

In recent decades, Majorca has become a hot tourist destination, particularly with Germans and Brits, who in high season can hop a direct flight to the Majorcan capital of Palma practically on the hour. But Nadal's Majorca hardly conforms to the "sun, surf, sex, and sangria" images of travel brochures and websites. The Nadal clan traces its roots on the island to the fourteenth century, and for generations the family has been a pillar of Manacor, a dusty, unprepossessing, landlocked town of thirty-five thousand, Majorca's answer to small-town America, a place where neighbors drop by unannounced and (not unlike Basel) the wealthy take pains to conceal their riches.

The current Nadal paterfamilias, also named Rafael, is a dignified man who was the longtime conductor of the local orchestra. He and his wife had three sons (Sebastian, Rafael, and Toni) and then a set of twins, a boy (Miguel Angel) and a girl (Marilen). The oldest son, Sebastian, began a successful real estate development and glass installation company. Need to negotiate a permit to build a seaside condo? You contact Sebastian. Need to install windows in your new hotel? Sebastian is your man. In 1986, Sebastian and his wife, Ana Maria, had their first child, a son, Rafael, nicknamed Rafa.

Federer's one-in-ten-billion talent and timing are the source of a fascinating cultural and genetic mystery. Nadal was about as close as you can get to being preordained for athletic success. Sebastian had the disposition for business and never much aptitude for sports, but his brothers were classic jocks. Miguel Angel Nadal was a fearsome soccer star who played in three World Cups for Spain and for the FC Barcelona team. On account of his bruising, hard-charging style, he earned the nickname "the Beast of Barcelona." Brother Rafael played second-division soccer and a bit of tennis. Toni, the cerebral brother with a fierce nonconformist streak, was a Balearic Islands Ping-Pong champion and a fine tennis player. Toni had too many other interests—history, philosophy, gardening, friends, general day-to-day curiosity—to devote himself fully to the sport, but he achieved a top-30 ranking in Spain and played cagey, tactical tennis at the level of, say, a strong college player in the United States.

Rafa was one of those athletic prodigies who combined precocity with ferocity. As early as anyone can recall, he seemed to have mastered the owner's manual for his body, knowing precisely what to do and where to go and which muscles worked how. But beyond that, he played sports—mostly soccer—with a ruggedness, a fearlessness, and an appetite for competition, especially when the opponents were bigger and older. When Rafa was three or four (accounts vary, and the subject himself pleads ignorance), Uncle Toni, then a pro at the local Manacor tennis club, equipped him with a racket. With shaggy hair moving with each stroke and a complexion matching that of the nitrate-colored clay underfoot, Rafa used his entire body to bat the ball over the net.

Toni was struck by his nephew's organic talent. Like a kid fiercely scribbling in a coloring book yet managing to stay inside the lines, Rafa could slug the ball with accuracy. But Toni was "probably more impressed," he says, with the kid's intensity. When Rafa was on the court, time became elastic. "Other boys, even much older, would hit the ball around and then get bored. Rafa would play and play until he was satisfied. Without anyone telling him, he would work on his weaknesses," says Toni. "Always, always, he had this discipline." Toni was happy to tutor his nephew but immediately established a few ground rules:

1. "If you ever throw a racket, we're finished. They're expensive, and when you throw a racket you don't just disrespect the sport, you disrespect all the people who can't afford equipment."

2. "Losing is part of competing. You will lose. And when you lose, it's not going to be my fault or the fault of your racket or the balls or the courts or the weather. It is your fault, and you will accept it. Too many people in this world make excuses for their problems. You take responsibility and try and do better next time. That's all."

3. "Have fun. When you stop enjoying this, it's no good. You'll find something else that gives you pleasure."

Like Federer, Nadal was also a talented soccer player, an aggressive striker who enjoyed the camaraderie of team sports. But he gravitated to tennis, fixated on the elemental challenge of hitting the ball hard enough to send it past the opponent, yet with enough control to maneuver it inside the lines. Nadal smacked the ball with two hands off both flanks. One day when Nadal was eight, Uncle Toni pulled him aside and asked, "How many tennis pros can you name who hit forehands with two hands?"

The kid thought about it. "Zero."

"Right," said Toni. "And you're not going to be the first."

In one of those small moments that would change the course of the sport, Toni encouraged Rafa to play tennis left-handed. Nadal was not classically ambidextrous: he used his right hand to do everything from writing his name to brushing his teeth to tossing darts. But Toni reckoned that since his nephew kicked a soccer ball pretty darn well with his left foot, maybe he could hit a tennis ball with his "off hand" too. Not only is tennis a sport that accords an inherent advantage to southpaws; Nadal's two-handed backhand would benefit from his powerful right arm. "I always hated playing lefties," recalls Toni. "I thought he should at least try it."

Without much complaint or adjustment, Nadal was soon smoking lefty forehands and serving with his off hand. He had a sidewinding style that enabled him to hit his shots with cartwheeling topspin, giving him a built-in margin of error. During the Punic Wars, Majorcan slingshot-wielding mercenaries helped the Carthaginian empire battle the Romans. Coincidence or not, Nadal's zinging forehand resembled that same slingshot motion.

When Nadal was eight, he won the Balearic tennis championships in the under-twelve division. A few years later, he was the champion in his age group for all of Spain. It was time for another Toni Nadal Life Lesson. Toni showed his nephew a list of the tournament's past winners. "How many names do you recognize?" he asked.

"Not many," Nadal responded with a shrug.

"Exactly," said Toni, leaving it to the kid to deduce that this junior title hardly guaranteed future success. A few months later, Nadal was the twelve-and-under champion for all of Europe.

The week Rafael turned twelve, Carlos Moya, also a Majorcan, won the French Open men's singles title. This was further proof that success was attainable.

Not that the kid needed the confidence boost. Part of the Nadal lore: Shortly after he won the French Open, Moya, a mentor figure to Nadal, pulled Rafa aside, prepared to deliver an inspiring if-I-can-do-it-you-can-too sermon. "What kind of tennis career do you envision having?" Moya asked him. "Would you like to have a career like mine?"

To this Nadal shook his head.

"No?" Moya said, surprised.

"No," said Nadal. "I want more."

Moya later told a Barcelona magazine that he knew right there that Nadal would become the better player.

While Federer enjoyed the social component of tennis, Nadal savored the competition. His opponent wasn't the ball or the laws of physics or the possibilities every shot presented; it was the hombre on the other side of the net. The opponent was there to be defeated. Nadal was never a menacing bully or a hothead or a poor sport. He just played as if losing a match carried a price in blood.

Quietly, Toni reckoned that his nephew was a potential adult champion. Less quietly, the Spanish Tennis Federation began inquiring about the kid. Might he like to leave his picturesque island and train at a national academy? Might he like to leave the comforts of his anonymous uncle and receive guidance from a big-name coach? The Nadal clan held an informal summit, not hard given that most of them lived in the same apartment building near Manacor's main square, each family inhabiting its own floor. In addition to teaching tennis, Toni was at the time a partner with Sebastian in the family business. The brothers quickly reached an agreement: Toni would keep his share of the business. But instead of working in the office, he would make training Rafael his full-time job.

In the retelling of the Rafael Nadal story, his parents tend to get short shrift, like characters in a TV drama cut out of the script. Their dignified refusal to trade on his celebrity or take public credit—or even give interviews—perpetuates this. But everyone in the Nadal family had a role in the creation of a champion. Ana Maria was the doting mother who made sure her son was well fed and did his homework and kept his room at least marginally clean. Sebastian was the pragmatic, hardworking father. Together they imparted values that borrowed heavily from the Calvinist handbook, emphasizing honesty, commitment, discipline, thrift, and the virtue of hard work.

They also provided the financial means, covering the travel and training costs. There's a misperception in sports that money dulls hunger, that the best athletes come from endemic poverty, as they somehow bring their struggles to bear on the field or court. The athletes from three-car-garage homes will be insufficiently motivated. But in the case of Nadal—and, for that matter, Federer—the opposite held true. Unencumbered by the pressure of feeling that the family's financial fortunes rested on whether they made it big, they could compete freely. The Nadals already had creature comforts, including a beach house on the Mediterranean coast. The Federers were ensconced in the Basel suburbs and vacationed in South Africa. If the prodigy kids wanted to follow their talents, great. If not, not.

Miguel Angel was the proverbial role model for Rafa. Not that the kid ever doubted his ability, but Uncle Miguel Angel was living proof that kids from Manacor with the Nadal DNA could indeed leave the island and become sports stars. By observing his uncle, Nadal internalized what he saw: how a professional athlete comports himself, how he trains, how he eats, how he handles both the benefits and the annoyances that attend fame. The rest of the clan formed a support group; in various configurations, they came to Rafael's matches to cheer him on. They clipped the newspaper articles for scrapbooks. They cooked him special meals before and after matches. Nadal says that this extended network managed to prop him up without spoiling him.

And still, it's hard to exaggerate the singular influence of Uncle Toni. Child psychologists often say that every adolescent male needs an adult to help him grow up, and it can't be a father. In Nadal's case, this was clearly his uncle, a mystical figure who shaped the kid's tennis game and his core identity in equal measure.

Nadal's sui generis tennis is often described as freakish and fluky in a raised-by-wolves kind of way. Prone as sports fans are to declaring that player X reminds them of player Y, one never hears this with respect to Nadal. There is practically nothing derivative about his game. The Spanish newspaper *El Mundo* once went so far as to editorialize: "Somewhere there was a Planet Nadal, where babies don't play with dolls but rackets, muscle grows before bone, courage is learned before speech and the heart beats faster. He is an adolescent who has transformed himself into a superman." But in truth, Nadal's game is the opposite of alien; it's homemade and meticulously hand-crafted. If you break down the many unconventional components of Nadal's strokes, Toni has an explanation for them all. Nadal's extreme western grip, with his hand almost perpendicular to the strings, nearly covering the butt of the racket handle? From his days as a Ping-Pong champ, Toni recognized the massive spin power you could create with this grip and transferred it to tennis. Nadal's elaborate follow-through that enables to him finish his strokes with the racket nearly brushing his skull? Since Rafael usually played opponents who were older and taller, he needed to hit high-bouncing, spin-slathered shots that offset any height disadvantage.

Tennis came easy to Rafael. Toni was there to make sure that nothing else did. He would make his nephew practice with dead balls and on pocked courts that gave dishonest bounces. Rafa would finish a practice and then, under his uncle's orders, sweep the clay court himself, a job usually left to low-paid attendants. Says Toni: "Just because you [excel] at hitting a tennis ball, that makes you no better or worse than anyone else." As a teenager, Rafael was given free shoes by Nike and Reebok, both of them vying for his endorsement. The first time Toni caught Rafael bending the heel and wriggling his foot into the shoes, he scolded, "You untie them and put them on properly and show respect. They may not cost you anything, but that doesn't mean they're not expensive." Leavening every victory with perspective, Toni compared success to shooting a gun. Even when you hit the target, there's that unpleasant recoil. "Everything positive in life," he says, "also has a negative side. That's why you shouldn't get too high or too low."

Toni practices the same themes of fierce independence and minimalist calm that he espouses. Though he has lived with the same woman for decades and together they are the parents of two children, he wears no wedding ring and does not refer to her as his wife. Why? "If I am friends with someone, I don't need to announce it. He knows, I know, and that's enough. We don't need [the label]. Same thing with my girlfriend." Though at times he speaks in Zen-like aphorisms, he has "zero" use for religion. "I don't believe. I studied history in the university, and I know that religion comes from ignorance of people. The great tribal societies, in those times when there was a ray of light, the people would blame it on a magician or whatever it was. When society moves forward and science moves forward, religion becomes less important. It's morality that is important, not religion."

Nadal had won the genetic Pick Six and fared well in the nurture department—what with his attentive, levelheaded parents, his mentoring uncle, his soccer star uncle, and a supportive extended family—but cultural forces also worked in his favor. For most of Spain's history, at least compared with other countries in western Europe, sports played a somewhat muted role in society. The odd torero or soccer player may have achieved a measure of fame, and that was about it. Through 1988, fewer Spanish athletes had won Olympic gold medals than their counterparts from Morocco, Finland, and New Zealand.

But owing to a mix of democracy, economic prosperity, and political stability, Spain quickly caught up. By 1992, Barcelona was a passionate and gracious host of the summer Olympic Games. Throughout the nineties, sports training centers and facilities were being built at a breakneck pace. *Marca,* a Madrid-based sports daily, became the country's largest newspaper. Predictably, as sports gained prominence in the national consciousness, Spain began minting Tour de France champions and NBA players and the winning soccer team in Euro 2008 competition. In tennis, between 1998 and 2003, three Spaniards—Moya, Albert Costa, and Juan Carlos Ferrero—won the French Open. As a Nike ad that ran in Spain during the summer of 2008, before the Beijing Olympics, put it: "Being Spanish is no longer an excuse, it's a responsibility."

Nadal caught the wave perfectly. Though he chose not to take advantage of the national tennis academy or state-sponsored coaching, he came of age at a time when sports funding was increasing dramatically. Plus, in Spain suddenly there was nothing considered more cool than being a sports star.

In 2001, the former champions Boris Becker and Pat Cash were scheduled to play an exhibition in Majorca. At the last minute, Becker withdrew with an injury. Desperate for a fill-in opponent, the organizer asked Cash if he would mind playing against the best local junior, a fourteen-year-old lefty, Rafael Nadal. Cash agreed and was impressed when the kid won a few early games. Then the kid won the first set, and Cash was no longer amused. Cash rallied to win the second set, fighting harder than he'd ever anticipated. The third set went to a tie-breaker. "I was like, 'Now this kid's gonna fold,'" recalls Cash. Except Nadal didn't, beating the 1987 Wimbledon winner. When word got out that Cash, then in his mid-thirties, had been beaten by a fourteen-year-old, he got a healthy ration of grief from his contemporaries. "I kept telling them, 'You don't understand. This kid is good,'" says Cash, who has, of course, since been vindicated.

Nadal's game evolved rapidly and in lockstep with his physique. By his mid-teens, he looked half man, half boy. He was nearing six feet in height, and his build was a straight Michelangelo job, all biceps and quads and perfect proportions. What little body fat Nadal had was concentrated in his cheeks, framing a jarringly boyish face. Nadal played in some international junior events, but his parents were concerned that the travel was affecting his schoolwork. Besides, there wasn't much competition.

He turned pro in 2001 and was able to skip the grueling rite of trolling the backwaters for ranking points at small challenger events. In April 2002, Nadal, then a fifteen-year-old phenom, played in the ATP event in Majorca and beat Ramon Delgado, a creditable top-100 pro at the time. In 2003, when Nadal was barely seventeen, younger than much of the field in the juniors draw, he reached the third round of Wimbledon—the youngest player to win two rounds at the All England Club since Boris Becker—and pierced the top 50 in the ATP rankings in the process.

The musclebound prodigy and his uncle made an odd pair, but the relationship worked. Nadal's grandfather tells the story that in one of Rafael's first pro matches, Toni told him: "Stay calm and relaxed. If things don't go well, I'll make it rain." Nadal trailed in the beginning but came back to even the match. Then it started raining. "You said you could make it rain," he told his uncle during the break in play. "If you can stop the rain, I can win."

When Rafael began winning, Sebastian suggested that his son start to pay for his coach from his own winnings and endorsement income. Toni rejected the idea immediately. Hell, he wasn't going to let any teenager sign his checks. "I don't want to receive money from [Rafa] because I want to be the boss," he says. "When I'm in business with the father, I don't need money from the boy. When the boy pays, I'm working for him, and that's not normal."

Unlike Federer, when Nadal came on the scene it was clear whom he would need to beat if he had designs on becoming Top Dog one day. Unless Nadal could figure out a way to combat Federer—displacing him from his comfort zone, hitting heavy topspin that frustrates a one-handed backhand, defending the court, jarring him with nonstop intensity—he would be another also-ran, left to tell his grandkids that he could have been a champion had his career not coincided with that of the Mighty Federer.

Nadal was still seventeen when he first faced Federer, who was already the world's No. 1–ranked player. Playing on the hard courts of the self-proclaimed "Fifth Slam," the 2004 Key Biscayne, Florida, event, Nadal thrashed Federer 6–3, 6–3. There were no signs of intimidation, no nervous yips from Nadal as he served out the match.

It was a considerable upset, especially given the surface. And yet Federer hardly appeared shellshocked by the result. "I've heard a lot about him and seen some matches of his," Federer said afterward. "I think this is not a big surprise for everybody." Asked to compare himself at age seventeen to Nadal, Federer had a quick and telling response: "He relies much more on his fighting spirit."

I interviewed Nadal in Rome in the spring of 2005. He was eighteen and was being tipped as the favorite to win the upcoming French Open. Earlier on the day we were to meet, Nadal had joined Andre Agassi to put on a tennis demonstration in St. Peter's Square. Over the previous ten days he'd earned in excess of $500,000 in prize money and was already being compensated handsomely to wear Nike apparel. Life was good. Yet he projected nothing resembling awe or the giddiness of the "pinch me" lottery winner. He perceived himself simply as the honest-working, talented athlete whose life was conforming to plan.

He came to the interview flanked by an ATP official cum emergency translator—a genial Spaniard named Benito Perez-Barbadillo, who would later become his personal media concierge—and his friend Feliciano Lopez, a strikingly handsome Spanish player. In my notes I had scrawled that Nadal appeared both older and younger than his chronological age. He joked with Lopez as some of the questions and answers awaited translation. At one point, he absent-mindedly detonated a zit on his thigh as he spoke.

Yet he made eye contact, offered a firm and earnest handshake, smiled abundantly, and, clearly a veteran of the media drill, answered in bland, inoffensive, impersonally polite sound bites. His goals? "Keep improving and keep working hard and keep being aggressive on the court." The biggest adjustments to playing professional tennis? "None, really. Missing my family, but I know they are always supporting me." Were it not for tennis, what would he be doing? "Hopefully playing soccer, no?" The facet of his game he'd most like to upgrade? "I am trying to improve everything. It can all get better, no?" (A friend of mine surmises that Nadal's habit of ending responses with "no?" is another manifestation of his on-court counterpunching.)

Recalling the Flaubert directive to "be regular and orderly in your life like a bourgeois, so that you may be violent and original in your work," Nadal is seldom described as anything other than normal or down-to-earth or modest. Even in Spanish, he rarely reveals much about himself or his interests outside tennis. His friends joke that his fallback gesture is an insouciant shrug. And when he blogs on his official website—an activity designed to convey color and personality—Nadal is so consistently bland that, on one post from 2008, he apologized to his fans, "I hope that I am not too boring."

Then, of course, the match starts and Nadal is thoroughly abnormal, rebellious, and resistant to convention.

The one time he was particularly animated was when discussing the tournament he'd most like to win. He began speaking faster than his words could be translated. "For sure, Wimbledon," he said through Perez-Barbadillo. "It means you are a true champion. For me, it's the ultimate tournament."

Nadal would win that Rome event, another $400,000 paycheck. A few weeks later, he would win his first French Open. By summer's end, he would establish himself as the World's Best Tennis Player Not Named Roger Federer. Though Nadal is at his best on clay, the notion that he is a typical Iberian "dirtballer" was quickly dismissed. By the time Nadal was twenty-one, he had won his third straight title at Roland Garros and reached his second straight Wimbledon final. It was clear he would inhabit the legends wing of the tennis pantheon. With the exception of Nadal's battle with a few nagging injuries, the first years of his career lacked the usual nodes and crests. It was a steady progression of triumphs.

As a young, handsome star athlete, Nadal had the world at the tips of his callused fingers. Yet he never showed interest in the trappings of success. While Federer is whisked to tournaments on private planes, as recently as 2008, Nadal flew back from the Australian Open in coach class. While Federer is a gastronome prone to raving about Gordon Ramsay or the previous night's sushi blowout, Nadal is happy ordering a room-service burger and sparking up his PlayStation. During the Beijing Olympics, Federer, citing privacy concerns, stayed at a luxury hotel in the city; Nadal not only stayed in the Olympic Athletes' Village, but other athletes nearly did a spit-take of their Gatorade when they saw him in the laundry room washing his own clothes. A few years ago at Roland Garros, Mats Wilander practiced with Nadal. After the session he turned to see his partner, the defending French Open champion, sweeping the court, an act tantamount to Wayne Gretzky's driving the Zamboni between periods.

During Wimbledon 2008, I mentioned to Perez-Barbadillo, Nadal's unofficial chief of staff, that Martina Navratilova used her prominence to support social causes and that Andre Agassi had donated tens of thousands to political candidates and causes, most of them left-leaning. I wondered if Nadal could have a similar impact in Spain. "It would never happen," Perez-Barbadillo said. "Rafa has his foundation, but he doesn't want to get involved like that. He thinks about issues, sure. But the less distractions the better."

While Federer was a citizen of the world, the king with the sprawling empire—the base in Switzerland, the foundation in South Africa, the American agent, the work with UNICEF—Nadal sought to disprove the adage that "no man is an island." At every opportunity, Nadal would return to Majorca, where to this day he lives in the apartment building the family shares. He has the same local girlfriend, fishing buddies, and golf partners. He still signs the guest register at the Club Tenis Manacor when he books a court, no different from the eleven-year-olds and ladies' league members. Though he owns a Mercedes, a prize for winning a tournament, he prefers to tool around the island in his Kia. Others in the tennis-sphere have tried to persuade Nadal to move his official residence to Monte Carlo or a similar tax haven. Federer keeps a stone and glass apartment in Dubai. Moya, the Majorcan, currently lists his residence as Geneva. Nadal has demurred. (As is the case when he plays, it's hard to maneuver him somewhere he doesn't want to go.) "I'm happy in Manacor. It's home. Why would I leave?"

On those rare instances when he's cosseted or given special dispensation, Uncle Toni is there to put him in his place. It drives Toni crazy. They go to Disneyland and they're told they can cut all the lines. They play golf and they're told they can feel free to drive their cart on the fairway. They go out for a bite to eat and they're told, thanks, but the meal is on the house. They go to the doctor and Nadal jumps to the front of the line. "It's not normal, everyone always telling you 'Yes, yes, yes,'" says Toni. "I am here to tell him 'No!' I'm here to challenge him to always say the opposite . . . Everyone tells him, 'You are very good.' I tell him always, 'Yes, you are very good, but I am more intelligent than you.'"

Not that Nadal rebels against these methods — *como se dice* "old school"? — or against the uncle who treats him like a mortal, not a demigod. "He is always going to be my uncle, and family is first," Rafa says. "And I am disciplined like him too, so I know where he's coming from."

When the run finally ends, Nadal will no doubt return to Manacor. He'll hang out with the same family and friends and eat the same food and keep the same routines. Toni too. Ever the Majorcan, he isn't particularly stressed about when that day might come. "When I go, I go," says Toni. "Maybe tomorrow we decide to go apart. If that's what Rafa would want, it would be fine with me. I'd be with my family and my garden."

How's that saying go? Oh, right. "The world follows its way. Don't worry, don't interfere, just relax and enjoy . . . And then one day you die."

The crowd was palpably uneasy as Federer served at 3–3. Nadal swiftly and methodically won the first three points, one with a dipping, flicking backhand passing shot that could not have been placed more accurately had he been armed with remote control. Federer was now down 4–6, 4–6, 3–3, 0–40. Given the difficulty Federer was having breaking Nadal's serve, this was the equivalent of triple match point. In Nadal's box, Uncle Toni chomped on his fingernails. The other entourage members looked at one another with eyebrows raised, as if to say, *This could be it.*

Unable to keep up any pretense of objectivity, a pair of

Spanish journalists in the press section gripped hands in happy anticipation. They had been writing about this curious left-handed kid for years. They'd seen him progress and win all those French Open titles. Now he was on the verge of winning Wimbledon.

This interval marked still another referendum on the players' mettle. And for the first time on this afternoon, it was Federer who had the more salient response. As he'd later confide to a friend, by this point he recognized that his Wimbledon reign might be drawing to a close, and he wasn't going down without a fight. No sense sparing the bullets now. He missed his first serve and slapped the errant ball away. His second serve kicked into Nadal's body. The return was a meek one, and Federer pounded a flat forehand.

Federer then unloaded a quartet of serves, none of which Nadal was able to put back in the court. Nadal would later concede with a shrug that he may have tightened up a bit here. But really, this was Federer at his finest. His serves weren't struck particularly forcefully, but each was well considered and well placed—Soft Power, as it were. When Federer saved the third break point by jamming a serve to Nadal's body, he pumped his fist and nodded to himself. The crowd thundered applause, less for the action than for Federer's intense reaction, a sign of just how invested he was in this performance. When he won the game and expelled a primal grunt, an elision of "Come on" that sounded like "Mmmmawn," the cheering spiked again.

In Federer's box, his girlfriend cupped her hands over her mouth and, having switched from English to French, yelled, "*Allez!*" While she may never have been in contention to win Grand Slam titles, Mirka had a deeper appreciation than most for what her boyfriend was enduring. Miroslava Vavrinec was born in the Slovakian part of Czechoslovakia in 1978. Two years later, seeking to flee Communist rule, the Vavrinec family immigrated to Switzerland. Mirka's parents ran a jewelry store in the town of Schaffhausen. In the late 1980s, the family attended a WTA event in Filderstadt, Germany, where they were introduced to Martina Navratilova, also a Czech émigré. Navratilova encouraged Mirka, then nine, to take up tennis. She complied. By fifteen, she was the Swiss junior champ. By twenty-one, she was a top-100 pro on the women's tour.

Vavrinec and Federer both represented Switzerland at the 2000 Olympic Games in Sydney. Though she was twenty-two and he was barely nineteen, they hung out together. Federer unexpectedly reached the semifinals before blowing a winnable match against Germany's Tommy Haas. He was crushed. "Now I have nothing to take home except my pride," he told reporters. But that wasn't entirely true. On the last night of the Games, he gathered the courage to kiss Vavrinec. The player who once vowed he would choose tennis over a girlfriend suddenly had one.

Their careers then veered in different directions. After reaching the third round of the 2001 U.S. Open, Vavrinec tore ligaments in her right foot and would never play at a high level again. Barely in her mid-twenties, she retired with unfulfilled goals and little in the way of prize money. But after several months of darkness, she became a vital member of Team Federer. As Federer evolved into a global star, Vavrinec took on the role of an executive, a chief of staff perhaps, in Roger, Inc. She handled interviews and scheduled appearances and helped build the Federer brand. Ambitious and businesslike, she helped him launch a signature RF cosmetics line. (It's hard to imagine that Federer, if left to his own devices, would promote an eponymous cologne redolent with "citrus chords and ozone elements with a hint of green tea.") She can even fill in capably when Federer needs a hitting partner.

The dynamic is fraught with potential conflicts — *Am I your girlfriend or your employee?* — but by all accounts and outward appearances, it has worked. Eight years into the relationship, Vavrinec circumnavigates the globe with Federer and sits in the stands during his matches, a BlackBerry all but surgically attached to her hands. She looks less like a standard sports girlfriend than a business manager. And her voice counts. She is the one who screens interview requests, who picks his U.S. Open "entrance music" (Rihanna's *Don't Stop the Music*), and who rejected an offer for Federer to read the top-ten list on David Letterman's *Late Show* because she deemed the content too sarcastic — after Federer had already arrived at the studio. To quote the T-shirts worn by a throng of Federer fans at the Monte Carlo event in the spring of 2008, "Mirka Is the Boss."

Rick Reilly, a former *Sports Illustrated* colleague of mine, met Federer for the first time in 2006 and was struck by his relationship with Vavrinec. As he wrote: "His hitting partner and his girlfriend are all the same person! And she's not even a lingerie model! Just an ordinary, very nice Swiss miss named Mirka. Derek Jeter has more babes than belts!"

Reilly had a point. It was Wilt Chamberlain who boasted of sleeping with more than ten thousand women. True or not, that the stat was not dismissed out of hand as implausible said plenty about a top sports star's access to, and appetite for, sex. Most athletes of far less stature than Federer — nubile twenty-somethings, dripping with disposable income — enjoy the sybaritic seductions of celebrity. (Old joke: What's the hardest thing about being a professional athlete? Trying to keep a straight face as you tell your girlfriend/wife you'll miss her before leaving on a road trip.) In tennis, there's a vibrant groupie culture: the circuit's traveling-road-show, if-it's-Tuesday-I-must-be-in-Montreal lifestyle is ideal for anonymous, or at the very least casual, sex. And then there's Federer. No Scandinavian models who walk into a room and reduce everyone else to trolls. No whispers of philandering. No paternity suits. Instead, a steady, mature, committed relationship with a Swiss woman three years his senior.

After both players held serve with ease, Federer led in the third set 5–4. At this point, the sky, already gunmetal gray, turned opaque. Drops of rain began pummeling the grass. It was a hell of a time for a delay, but it wasn't altogether unwelcome. Such dramatic sports-theater called for an intermission.

Though, mercifully, there had been only a few "suspensions of play" in 2008, the rain delay is a Wimbledon bedrock. And everyone knows the Kabuki ritual. The team of seventeen groundskeepers works with military precision to unfurl a green nylon tarp over the court, while the crowd lets out a collective "AWWWwwwww" and an arsenal of umbrellas quickly pop open in the stands. The club members retreat to indoor lounges and covered balconies. The sodden masses put on their plastic ponchos and walk the grounds. Many amble over to the beer concession for pints of liquid fortification. A brave few gather at what, by definitional courtesy, is called a "food court" underneath Centre Court.

For all its virtues, Wimbledon surely provides the worst ballpark concessions in sports, a superlatively awful mix of oil-spill pizza, malodorous puddings, sweaty sausages, and pastries stuffed with assorted mystery meats and gelatinous fillings which conform to every tired stereotype of British cuisine. Never mind the absence of stadium naming rights or courtside signage; perhaps the tournament's real loss of revenue comes from an insistence on serving food unfit for human digestion.

Journalists on deadline dash to the pressroom to begin out-lining their stories—in this case, cheating by beginning their accounts of Nadal's straight-set Wimbledon victory. Broad-casters step out of their booths, relishing their first bathroom break and breath of fresh air in hours. The white-attired line judges head to the quaintly named "officials' buttery," a lounge where, a friend of mine jokes, margarine is strictly forbidden.

As for Federer and Nadal, they hustled off the court and into the clubhouse. Federer methodically gathered his racket bag and his white leather man-purse; Nadal simply slung his duffel over his sweaty shoulder. As Federer trudged to the locker room, a source recalls that he was intercepted in front of the door by Mirka, who had bolted from her seat to meet him. According to one observer, she radiated a calm intensity as she delivered a forceful pep talk, gripping Federer's arms and reminding him that he, not Nadal, was the five-time champ. The observer says that Federer listened in solemn silence and nodded sheepishly.

Ordinarily, a player would use this opportunity to consult with a coach. But Federer had no such aide-de-camp on the payroll. Tennis coach is one of the more peculiar lines of work. It can be a demanding job—all that time spent deconstruct-ing strategy, all those hard miles invested on the practice court, all those late nights scouting opponents. Then, at the moment of truth, the match begins and the coaches sit in the stands, dark sunglasses wrapped around their faces, often still as gar-goyles, betraying no emotion lest they violate tennis's strict rules against . . . coaching.

Since parting with Peter Lundgren, Federer has essen-tially been self-coached. In fact, the joke in the locker room is that Federer is coached by the IBM match statistics sheets that he reads after he's done playing. The closest he came to a coach was a sporadic, part-time arrangement with Tony

Roche, a terse and reserved Aussie almost forty years Federer's senior. (For the 2008 European clay court campaign and
for his first few matches at Wimbledon 2008 he worked with
Jose Higueras, the former Spanish pro.) Federer reckons that
he's smart enough to devise his own strategy, and motivated
enough to run his own practices. "Solving the riddles" by himself, he says, provides an added source of confidence.

That decision was famously validated at the 2005 Wimbledon final when Federer spent a rain delay fashioning a strategy that enabled him to beat Andy Roddick, by disrupting
Roddick's rhythm with more frequent attacking, more storm-
ing of the net. At the time, Roddick was coached by the well-
regarded, well-compensated Brad Gilbert; the conventional
wisdom was that Federer had not only outplayed the player
but had outcoached the coach that day.

In the locker room, Nadal had positioned himself in such a
way that he could see Federer but Federer could not really see
him, another incremental mental edge. Nadal sat alone for a
moment but was soon joined by Uncle Toni and Maymo, the
Majorcan whom Nadal had hired as a full-time physiotherapist. After confirming that, yes, Nadal's right knee felt okay
and that, no, he wasn't dehydrated, there wasn't much else left
to say. Nadal had played a near-flawless match. Unflustered on
the important points, he was beating Federer mentally. Barring a colossal collapse or comeback—neither scenario worth
mentioning or contemplating right now—Nadal was on the
cusp of winning Wimbledon for the first time.

Maymo went to work kneading Nadal's muscles. Although
stress hormones have the effect of relaxing the body and acting
as anti-inflammatories, they are also catabolic substances that
can break down muscle tissue, compounding the wear and
tear on the muscles caused by exertion. The massage is an attempt to bring fresh circulation, blood that contains proteins

and lipids. Not surprising given Nadal's game, Maymo spent more time on his employer's legs and feet than on his arms and shoulders. With nothing to do and not much to say with Rafael three games from victory, Uncle Toni closed his eyes and took a nap, a Spanish siesta.

Federer tried to remind himself that he rallied before from two sets down to beat Nadal (in Miami in 2005), and he could do so again. And he, too, underwent a massage at the hands of his physiotherapist, Gary Hamilton. A thickly built Australian with intensely green eyes, Hamilton had run a remedial massage therapy business out of his home in Wonthaggi, a coal-mining town eighty miles south of Melbourne. In 2007, he received a call asking if he could work his magic in the locker room of the Australian Open. One of his first days on the job, Hamilton found himself rubbing Federer's lats, glutes, and calves. Federer apparently thought highly of the massage; in the spring of 2008, he summoned Hamilton to work for him privately. By the start of Wimbledon, Hamilton had been on the job eight weeks. One day he was working on the pulled muscles of Australian high school cricketers; the next day he was part of Team Federer, staying in Europe's finest hotels, flying on private planes to Monte Carlo and Paris and Hamburg.

Hamilton hadn't seen his wife and two sons in months. They were planning to join him after Wimbledon for a family vacation in Europe. Then Hamilton would return to work, following Federer to tournaments in Toronto and Cincinnati and the Beijing Summer Olympics. It was a fluke opportunity, he was the first to admit, and who knew how long it would last? But here it was the first week of July and Hamilton had already decided that it had been the best summer of his life.

Though only a handful of players can afford to hire a private physiotherapist, it is less an extravagance than a sound financial investment. Hamilton politely declined to discuss his salary. But for the sake of argument, let's assume a ballpark figure of $5,000 a week, including expenses. In 2008, Federer earned $6 million in prize money for the nineteen tournaments he entered, an average of $315,000 per event. Nadal would earn more, nearly $6.8 million over eighteen events, roughly $375,000 a pop. If a physio's magic fingers enabled a top player to remain healthy and enter one additional event (or prevented one additional withdrawal), it was a worthwhile outlay. If a physio could play some small role in helping a client to win the Wimbledon title . . . well, that would be priceless.

As the players sought sanctuary in the locker room, in NBC's courtside booth John McEnroe and his broadcast partner, Ted Robinson, both native New Yorkers, passed the time by imitating the distinctly nasal voice of Marv Albert, the seminal New York sports announcer. (McEnroe: "Kick save and a beauty by Giacomin!" Robinson: "DeBusschere to Bradley to Reed—and one!") Waiting for play to resume, the NBC network cut to a series of commercials. The first spot featured Boris Becker hitting a tennis ball. Becker's voice kicks in: "How did I miss dis? Da adrenaline. Da vill ta vin. Da fahn." Becker then crashes through a wall and, dressed as a James Bond manqué, lands at a card table to announce, "Pokah iss my new game." The ad is for pokerstars.net, which, as the small no-purchase-necessary-void-where-prohibited disclaimer informs viewers, is "not a gambling website."

If there's something a bit unseemly about a former top sportsman endorsing on-line games of chance, at least there is a real honesty to the ad. Truth is, a legion of former athletes in their postcareer afterlives struggle to replicate the surge—*da adrenaline, da vill ta vin*—that athletic competition once provided them. Becker, a bit of a lost soul since his retirement, has been outspoken on this very point. And the shame of it is that the erratic jolts of gambling are the closest a lot of ex-jocks come to replicating the rhythms and chemical rushes of athletic competition.

An odd bit of juxtaposition, the following thirty-second spot was a commercial for Rolex watches featuring Federer. As earnest orchestral music plays, a brief Federer "Wimbledon greatest hits" highlight reel is interspersed with footage of a rotating watch. The spot ends with tolling bells as Federer hoists the Wimbledon trophy. Most folks who watch too much tennis have seen this ad countless times, and it's interesting on a few fronts. For one, it's worth noting that Federer does no acting or speaking. This ad required no apparent time commitment on his part, no days spent on a studio set, detracting from his tennis.

More than that, this commercial runs counter to the longtime jock-ad philosophy. For years, companies selling goods and services, from vegetable soup to cologne to corrective vision surgery, have enlisted athletes to help move product. The basic tenet, of course, is one of association: if Famous Athlete uses this brand of pain reliever, Joe Consumer will want to as well. But in addition to the fees they can derive, athletes get something else out of the deal: they can use the opportunity as a thirty-second commercial for themselves. The message distills to, "Cheer for me, because were it not for my superior fast-twitch muscle fibers, I'd be just like you." Instead of stressing exceptionalism, the ads almost always emphasize Everyman sensibilities. Arnold Palmer has to change his motor oil just like you and I do. Michael Jordan is reduced to a guy in his Hanes underwear, the clod who gets mustard on his chin, eats McDonald's, and uses MCI to place long-distance calls. O. J. Simpson—pre-devil-incarnate phase—ran undignified through airports to catch his flight and get to his Hertz rental car. (No NetJets and waiting limo for him.) A perennial series of Miller beer ads existed on the premise that athletes are boobs afflicted with terminal cases of arrested development. In what is perhaps the quintessential jock ad, the Pittsburgh Steelers' fearsome Mean Joe Greene is disarmed by a young kid who plies him with the same bottle of Coca-Cola available to anyone with a few loose quarters.

Yet here's Federer, not only endorsing watches that cost as much as midpriced cars, but doing so in a way that emphasizes his superiority. This isn't Everyman. It's Superman, a handsome athletic being on a grass tennis court moving gracefully to deifying classical music. Good for Federer, I always thought. Good for him for keeping his authenticity and forgoing the easy self-effacement or the message of "Hey, pal, let's grab a beer and get to know each other!" But as for the mystery of why he hasn't been better able to penetrate the American mass market, well, look no further.

The rain subsided after a bit more than an hour, the typical length of a Wimbledon delay. Called back to the court, Nadal and Federer went through a cursory warm-up. Nadal again indulged his tics, adjusting his socks and puttering around with his water bottles, though Federer was already waiting and the umpire has already intoned "Time." "It's not superstition. I know it doesn't affect whether the ball is going to go for a winner or an error," Nadal says. "But it seems like the routine makes me feel more concentrated."

Here's another earmark of elite pro athletes: their rhythm isn't easily interrupted. Despite the lengthy delay, both Federer and Nadal quickly resumed their unsurpassed play. Withstanding several moments of incandescence from Federer, Nadal held serve. 5–5. Sports shrinks frequently speak of athletes' achieving "tunnel vision," undeterred by anything on the periphery; a more accurate term in tennis might be "funnel vision." Ideally, players cast a wide gaze at their opponent, narrowing their focus only when the ball arrives. Studying the opposition, players sometimes notice the slightest mannerism —a "tell," they call it in poker—that they can use to their advantage. Pete Sampras, for instance, was once able to discern that as Boris Becker began his service motion, he unconsciously pointed his tongue in the direction he was about to serve. At this point deep in the third set, Federer and Nadal spent considerable time looking over the net, hoping to uncover some incremental benefit.

At 6–6, they began a tiebreaker, a high-stakes winner-take-all shootout, said winner being the first player to earn at least seven points by a two-point margin. Wimbledon first instituted the tiebreaker in 1971, but it kicked in only when games were tied at eight. In 1979, the tournament changed the rule to commence a tiebreaker at six games all, except for the final set, when the winner must prevail by two games. (We will comply with the unwritten tennis edict that at Wimbledon, no tiebreakers are allowed to be described without first offering homage to the John McEnroe–Bjorn Borg tiebreaker in the fourth set of the 1980 final. It spanned twenty-two thrilling minutes and ended with McEnroe staving off a half-dozen match points and winning 18–16. The "Battle of 18–16," as it's been sentimentalized, is so deeply embedded in tennis lore that it is all too easy to forget that Borg recovered and won that match.) The tiebreaker looms particularly large at Wimbledon, where the serve is broken so infrequently, and it has figured heavily in Federer's success. Of the last twenty-five tiebreakers Federer had played at Wimbledon, he'd won twenty-two, two of which were in the 2007 final against Nadal. The message: *You might hold your serve for an entire set, but when we get to six all and every point counts, my superiority will become apparent.*

Federer began with a nasty serve that not only tattooed the center line but then hooked, unreturnably, into Nadal's body. Though Federer lost the next point when he misfired on a backhand, it was a bold offensive shot that he didn't much mind missing. He continued the aggressor—*If I'm going down, I'm going down swinging*—and began hitting his targets, painting the corners of those symmetrical Mondrian rectangles on the court. Rotating his body in midair, a testament to that core strength, he smoked a pair of inside-out forehands for winners, swinging one way while his entire body drifted the other and somehow making it all look natural. In a vacuum, these were glorious shots. In the pressure of the third set of a Wimbledon final, they were breathtaking. After nine points, Federer was ahead 6–3, one point from extending the match to a fourth set.

Nadal momentarily stopped Federer's run with some courageous play of his own. At 6–5, Federer prepared for one of the more critical points of his career. He toweled off, selected a ball, and went into his service motion. Federer tossed the ball upward and reached for it, briefly putting his belly and belt on full display. When the ball was at its apex, he struck it near the top of his racket. The ball sailed over the net at "just" 115 mph, slowing to roughly half that speed by the time it bounced. But Federer had guided the ball to the corner of Nadal's service box, out of reach. An ace, placed with geometric perfection.

The crowd's roar thickened with approval during another impromptu standing O. All those Pimm's-drinking patricians were now going positively apeshit, the chants of "Rajah-Rajah-Rajah!" suffocating "Rafa-Rafa-Rafa!" Whenever tennis matches are pushed to additional sets, announcers invariably enthuse, "The fans want more tennis!" But this went far beyond a desire for an additional set of tennis at no extra charge. The champ had been battered in the early rounds by the pugnacious newcomer. Now he was fighting back.

Federer's reaction to winning the set was subdued: a firm fist-clench and a quiet "yeah." Nadal shook his head to suggest "too good." At her apartment in Wimbledon, Venus Williams exhaled, knowing there was at least another set of tennis to play before she readied herself for the Champions Ball. As NBC went to a commercial and the cameras panned to Federer and his elated supporters, a quick-thinking NBC audio technician scrambled to punch up the Pearl Jam chorus "I'm Still Alive."

Fourth Set

6–7

FEDERER WAS A SLIGHT favorite with the oddsmakers when the match began, 1.8 to Nadal's 2.2. Which is to say, $1 waged for Federer would have returned 80 cents in profit had he won, whereas $1 waged for Nadal would have yielded $1.20 profit. But now, with Nadal still leading two sets to one, the odds were tilted heavily in the Spaniard's favor.

Sports and gambling are inextricably linked, sports being one of the few forms of live entertainment that features unpredictable, irregular outcomes. (Plus, most fans feel, secretly anyway, that they have special expertise; and besides, is speculating on the Super Bowl outcome any worse than speculating on, say, oil futures or pork bellies?) But to traffic in understatement, in the past, the Vegas sports books had never been brimming with tennis action. Who—formally or informally, legally or illegally—bet big bucks on tennis? True, until recently some tournaments, including Wimbledon, offered on-site betting parlors, but they were often the provinces of coaches, trainers, journalists, and others with backstage access, eager to capitalize on inside information. They'd overhear that some Slovenian was receiving heavy-duty treatment for a back injury and plop down $20 on the guy to lose, figuring the ill-gotten gains would cover their bar tab that night.

The Internet changed all that. Suddenly it was possible for anyone, anywhere, at any time to put down a wager on a tennis match. The tennis bum willing to bet that Sampras would beat Agassi, but unwilling to associate with the Mob-affiliated knee breaker in the Camaro? He now need only let his browser do the work. Today tennis is, improbably, the world's third-largest betting sport after horseracing and soccer.

The shotgun marriage between tennis and gambling was made all too apparent shortly after Wimbledon in 2007, when Nikolay Davydenko, a Russian pro bearing an uncanny resemblance to a baby chick, what with his small head and fuzzy blond hair, entered a whistle-stop ATP tournament in Sopot, Poland. Davydenko, then ranked fourth in the world, faced Martín Vassallo Argüello, a subjourneyman from Argentina. The curious arc and outcome of this nothing match would soon become as familiar to tennis fans as a Wimbledon final.

Before the first ball was struck, Davydenko went from being a heavy, 5-to-1 favorite—as well he should have been—to being an underdog. Weird. While a match of such little consequence would ordinarily generate a volume of around $750,000 in bets, this encounter yielded roughly $7 million, most of the money laid down by a half-dozen individuals. Weirder still. Then, when Davydenko won the first set, yet more bets came in *backing* Vassallo Argüello, who—surprise, surprise—took the second set and then the match when Davydenko retired on account of a foot injury. Clearly, something was rotten in Sopot.

The wagering was not done through shadowy bookies or at OTB parlors. It was done on-line, mostly through Betfair, a British firm. Given the highly irregular betting patterns, Betfair took the unprecedented step of voiding all bets. It then

alerted the ATP of this most suspicious result. Though the
ATP would eventually "exhaust all avenues of inquiry and
find no evidence of violation" by either Davydenko or Vassallo
Argüello — a vital semantic difference from altogether exonerating the players — unanswered questions remained. Why
did Davydenko deny investigators access to the cell-phone records of his brother and wife? Why did Davydenko wait until
the third set — by which time the bets had cleared — to retire?
And those "winning" bettors whose tickets had been unilater-
ally, abruptly annulled, why were they not clamoring to receive their millions?

For all the unpleasantness generated by the scandal, at least
it offered a window into the new frontiers of sports betting. If
television is the engine that drives the Sports Industrial Complex, gambling is the backup generator. Since so much sports
wagering is done illegally and informally, reliable figures are
hard to come by, but conservatively, sports gambling is a $100
billion global business. By 2010, half of that is expected to be
done over the Internet.

In this brave new wagering world, Betfair is the gaming industry's answer to the heroin needle swap or the free condoms
at a nightclub. That is, if you're going to engage in morally
questionable behavior, at least be safe about it. The company's
slogan is "Betting as it should be." Founded by a pair of former London investment bankers, Betfair operates as a stock
exchange for sports bets. Bettor A makes his offer. *Federer to
beat Nadal.* If an offsetting bet can be found — *Nadal to beat
Federer* — great. If there's no offsetting bet, the offer dies. And
because it's all on-line, wagers can be made in real time, even
after events have started. It's an exercise more akin to eBay or
on-line dating than to a bookie handing out betting slips. Betfair simply provides the service, the server, and the software,
albeit for a two to five percent fee. Like all bookies, Betfair

tries to match supply with demand. The difference is that, by using computers rather than people, Betfair's risk threshold is essentially zero.

Headquartered just a few miles from the All England Club in the village of Hammersmith, on the banks of the Thames River, Betfair is your typical thriving Internet start-up. The workforce, which exceeded 1,200 in the summer of 2008, is made up mostly of twentysomethings in T-shirts and jeans, their faces glowing before an unending constellation of LCD screens. Betfair's revenue has grown nearly eightfold—from $64 million in 2003 to a projected $500 million in 2008. There is a branch office in Australia, and the company has plans to expand to the United States and China. In January 2008, the Tokyo Stock Exchange closed early because the 4.5 million trades executed that day overwhelmed its computer system. That same day, Betfair executed 5.5 million transactions.

If the bad news is that technology has made sports gambling (and the perils that go with it) more accessible than ever, the good news is that, because of the same technology, it's never been easier to detect corruption. And because Betfair is indifferent to the outcome of events, it's happy to share its information with governing bodies. In the case of Davydenko, Betfair happily turned over all its evidence to the ATP—who bet, when they bet, where they bet, their computers' IP numbers and payment methods, their betting histories. It also helped the ATP and an anticorruption task force to analyze the wagering on hundreds of matches over the past five years. The task force concluded that forty-five matches "had unusual betting patterns that require further review to ascertain if they affected the integrity of professional tennis or if there were other reasons for the outcome of the matches." It's worth pointing out that this independent review found no evidence of corruption in tennis or links to organized crime. But the investigators made fifteen recommendations to the ATP, all of which were accepted and adopted.

Tennis is singularly well suited to outcome-fixing: the players are individual contractors who need not conspire with teammates before throwing a match, nor answer to angry coaches and owners afterward. Even the best players commit dozens of unforced errors every time they take the court. Who's to say whether a player tanks (loses on purpose) or simply gets beat? (Certainly not the ATP officials who, irony of ironies, docked the embattled Davydenko $2,000 for "lack of best effort" in October 2007, only to rescind the fine on appeal.) And many minor events lack television coverage, so there is often no video evidence of the match for investigators to analyze.

If there's a saving grace to a match-fixing scandal, it is that the allegations seemed limited to second-rate players at second-rate events. Still, nothing will doom a sport faster than a perception that the competition isn't honest. In the wake of *l'affaire* Davydenko, tennis authorities went into high dudgeon. Players caught wagering on any matches were fined and suspended. At Wimbledon, players were warned that match-throwing risked a two-year prison term. Tournaments refused to issue official credentials unless the bearer pledged not only to refrain from gambling but to report suspicious gambling-related activity. They also blocked access to gambling websites on the grounds. Locker room security, once laissez faire, became so tight that even Rafael Maymo, Nadal's trusted physiotherapist, was denied entry into the seeded players' enclave during the first week of Wimbledon.

This response has stemmed gambling among the insiders. But it also became clear that tennis, like all sports, is ultimately helpless to stop any sports fan with a DSL line and a few bucks to burn. Consider that during the entire 2006 World Cup soccer tournament, Betfair handled £64 million in bets. During the Nadal-Federer match alone, Betfair would put up £49,137,328 (then worth close to $100 million) in the match-odds market. For Betfair, it was a record for a single sporting event.

As the fourth set began, Nadal was subject to one of the cruelties of tennis. A few minutes earlier, he needed only to win a tiebreaker to become the Wimbledon champ; suddenly he needed to win another set. There are no knockouts in tennis, no walk-off home runs or Hail Mary touchdowns. It's an incremental sport—"brick by brick," Andre Agassi once put it —and, barring injury, there's no way to win except cumulatively.

Still, Nadal claims that this dispiriting truth never infected his thinking. "I didn't let myself think about that. There was nothing I could do about it, so [why] waste [energy]? . . . I never thought I was going to lose, so it was okay." He betrayed no outward signs of disappointment; his disposition and thousand-yard stare were indistinguishable from when he was winning. Nadal christened the fourth set with a breezy service game.

It was around this time that Diane Morales stopped watching the match on the TV in her Memphis, Tennessee, home. A fifty-eight-year-old high school Spanish teacher, Morales had been a casual tennis fan until 2005 when her daughter told her, "There's this Spanish kid who's going to win the French Open." Morales caught a glimpse of Nadal and has been—um, how to put this?—a spirited fan ever since. "It wasn't even a physical thing, but it was this visceral reaction where I couldn't take my eyes off him," she says. "He's so adorable, so passionate, so different from the other players. Rafa is so *alive.*"*

Morales soon began adorning the walls of her classroom in the Memphis suburb of Germantown with Nadal posters. And she learned that she wasn't alone in her reaction. Thousands of others scattered all over the globe shared her Rafaphilia. These tribalists meet at vamosbrigade.com, an unofficial Nadal website, which is not to be confused with his official, far more bland, Nike-sponsored site, rafaelnadal.com. Vamosbrigade.com is administered by four women who, in the spirit of the borderless Internet, are based in France, Germany, Wallingford, England, and Baton Rouge, Louisiana. For the shared server fee of $13 a month, they have created a fan club, a destination where thousands converge to discuss their favorite player. There are match updates and an article archive, a cheering thread during each Nadal match and a "fan art" section where Rafaelites can post their renderings. There's even a "droolers anonymous" link, a repository for lubricious thoughts and fantasies. The posts are in English, but various volunteers translate the content into six languages. Most of the site's two thousand registered members have never met Nadal. Some have never seen him play live. Few have ever met face to face. But the bonds are sufficiently strong that members will IM one another during Nadal's matches. If on-line wagering is the Internet at its most destructive, one could make the case that this is the connective power of the Web at its finest.

Soon after Morales discovered the site, she was logging on to vamosbrigade.com first thing every day. Under the nom de

---

* To one detached observer, this seems to be a common response. Nadal has immense appeal among older women, but they adore him as they would a cute younger brother, not a Brad Pitt.

net "Daylily," she writes effusive posts about Nadal. When another poster affectionately referred to Morales as "*la Meiga*"
("sorceress" or "witch" in Spanish), she played along. Whenever Nadal competes in an important match, Morales pretends
to stir a cauldron she calls "Bubbles," concocting a brew that
will bring Nadal good luck. When Nadal faces Andy Murray of
Scotland, for instance, Morales might throw sheep's belly into
the mix. When Nadal is pitted against Novak Djokovic, she
might add porcupine quills, symbolic of the player's spiky hair.
Every brew contains cinnamon, Nadal's "lucky spice." Clearly,
she's among the twenty percent of American sports fans who,
according to a recent Associated Press poll, "do things in hopes
of either improving the fortunes of their favorite teams or
averting a curse on them."

Morales had been watching the Wimbledon final alongside her daughter—who named her Lexus sedan "Rafa"—a
pair of tennis-seein' Tennesseans, if you will. They periodically
logged on to the vamosbrigade.com cheering thread to take
part in the group therapy sessions during the match. But as the
momentum whipsawed back to Federer, both women decided
they were jinxing the result. They cleaned the house during
the fourth set, glancing only occasionally at the score on-line.

Federer responded to Nadal's strong first game, squeezing off
another round of well-placed serves and forehands. As Nadal
tried to pick apart Federer's backhand, he encouraged Federer
to counter tactically by "running around" his backhand and
pummeling inside-out forehands. *Maybe now you'll think twice
about playing to that side of the court, buddy.* On the third point
of Federer's service game, he lasered three such inside-out
beauties, splaying his legs and lifting both feet off the ground
as he hit the ball. The last of these shots streaked past Nadal
for 40–0.

(Digression: In tennis's scoring system—which, like so much about the sport, is either cloyingly old-fashioned or endearingly quaint, depending on your point of view—the term "love" is thought to derive from the French word for egg, *l'oeuf*, the zero resembling the shape of an egg. The other scores were supposed follow a clock, and the player who claimed four points, or got to sixty minutes, would win the game. So why "40" and not "45"? Unclear, though according to one theory, in the Middle Ages the number "45" represented prostitution—much the same way 666 denotes Satan—which offended the sensibilities of priggish tennis officials. The less sexy explanation is that "45" was originally used, but over the years was abbreviated to "40.")

Had this been boxing, the early fourth set would have represented the middle rounds, when exhausted combatants clutch and grab, waiting desperately for a second wind. Nadal and Federer, though, kept slugging, somehow ratcheting up the quality of their play in proportion to the drama of the match. On one point, Nadal would rip a did-you-see-that? winner, painting the corner with a backhand he had struck from a few yards behind the court. On the following point, Federer would conjure a comparably dazzling shot. Tennis statistics tend to have limited value, as "winners" and "unforced errors" are subjective determinations—especially since, with both players retrieving so adeptly, it often took the equivalent of a half-dozen winners to prevail in a single point. But the overwhelming majority of the points were being earned by acts of commission and not omission. By 1–1 in the fourth set, Federer and Nadal combined had more than twice as many winners as errors, empirical support for what everyone already knew viscerally: this was one hell of a match.

As they paced around the court between points, both players radiated intensity. While this may be Nadal's trademark expression on the court, Federer usually projects a calmness that can bleed over into transparent enjoyment. Vic Braden, the prominent tennis coach and psychologist, had recently attended a seminar given by Dr. Gerard Medioni, a University of Southern California computer science professor. Medioni spoke about the intelligence experts who use facial expressions to finger terrorists. Braden decided to apply similar techniques to tennis. After watching DVDs of Federer's matches frame by frame, Braden noticed something unusual. Against all other opponents, Federer plays with his eyes wide open, focuses straight ahead, and with his mouth turned upward. But when he faces Nadal—and only Nadal—he tends to frown and look downward. And it wasn't just when he was losing. Braden saw that Federer assumes this facial expression even in warm-ups, before the match has started. Never mind the well-lubricated sports cliché that Nadal was "in Federer's head." He was in his face too.

This recalled John McEnroe's never losing his famous temper when he faced Bjorn Borg, or Chris Evert's uncharacteristic nervous giggles before she played Martina Navratilova, or Larry Bird's going for a pregame jog in the arena parking lot before meeting Magic Johnson and the Lakers. A departure from standard operating procedure is just part of the unique thermodynamics of a rivalry, one of the stranger relationships in sports.

The Federer-Nadal rivalry unofficially took hold in the spring of 2006, and it came not a moment too soon. The gladiatorial nature of tennis makes it well suited to rivalries. In fact, in the absence of a rivalry, the sport suffers. McEnroe and Borg played each other only fourteen times (fittingly, each won seven matches), but their relationship was so textured, their contrasts so stark, that they led tennis through a golden age. After Borg exited tennis—in no small part because of the claustrophobic effects of the McEnroe rivalry—even the highest-stakes men's matches could seem hollow, mere sporting events and not broader, deeper tableaux. Pete Sampras and Andre Agassi had the makings of a gripping rivalry but were never really able to synchronize their best years. For various reasons, other combinations and permutations—Marat Safin v. Gustavo Kuerten, Lleyton Hewitt v. Andy Roddick, Roddick v. Federer—never yielded a sustained rivalry either.

But then came Federer-Nadal, which, on its face, meets all the prerequisites of a compelling rivalry:

- They represent different countries and cultures and value systems.
- They play often.
- They reveal their true selves when they compete.
- Their games are vastly different, two men armed with different sets of tools trying to achieve the same objective.
- They are both in their prime.
- They are the best in the game. Together they had come to form an oligarchy that had the effect of disenfranchising the rest of the field. Nadal was ranked lower but, perversely, won the majority of their encounters, creating an odd twist, the number two guy beating the number one guy: the player touted as the GOAT unable to beat the opponent ranked below him.

It took time for Federer to warm to the concept of having a nemesis, a player against whom he'd be judged (and it's still not clear that he completely relishes the rivalry). When first asked about Nadal, Federer quickly grouped him with another half-dozen challengers. Standing in direct conflict with a colleague ran counter to Federer's tennis worldview. But when it became clear that Nadal was *the* player who was going to probe the limits of his game and his character, Federer accepted the rivalry and then broke out the Soft Power.

Most incumbent stars in Federer's position would have "big-dogged" the new kid, putting him through the equivalent of a fraternity hazing. Federer took the opposite approach. When he spoke (glowingly) of Nadal, he always called him by the diminutive nickname "Rafa." He slapped five with Nadal as they passed in the locker room. He invited Nadal aboard his private plane, and they flew to a tournament together. In 2005, Nadal came to Federer's hometown of Basel for the ATP event. Sidelined with a foot injury at the time, Federer nonetheless showed up at Nadal's hotel room unannounced just to say *hola*. As recently as 2007, Federer walked into a locker room and saw Nadal juggling a soccer ball, part of his post-match cooldown regimen. Federer cast him an amused look. Nadal nodded and kicked the ball to Federer. Together they kicked the ball back and forth, chatting casually. "Hey," gushed Federer, "you're better than Maradona!"

Nadal, too, needed to grow into the rivalry. He downplayed the relationship at first, then traversed the fine line between deference and obsequiousness. More than once, Nadal administered a brutal beating to Federer on the court but then promptly declared the man he had just beaten the Greatest Player Ever. In 2007, Nadal agreed to appear in a hagiographic Federer documentary—a telling decision in itself—and, smiling as if in awe, he summarized his rival's game thusly: "He's the perfect player. Perfect serve. Perfect volley. Super-perfect forehand. Perfect backhand. Very fast on court. Everything is perfect." (*Perfect?* Try to envision, at the height of their rivalry, Ted Williams describing Joe DiMaggio as the "perfect baseball player.") Nadal began referring to Federer first by the nickname "Rogelio" and then "Numero Uno." As Federer said

of Nadal in 2008 when asked about the level of respect he per-
ceives from his rival, "He always thinks I'm the greatest."

Even after he pasted Federer in the 2008 French Open final, Nadal went happily back to playing Salieri to Federer's
Mozart. After the match I asked Nadal if he truly didn't consider himself the best player in the world now. He shrugged
and shook his head. "No, no, no. I feel like number two now,"
he said. "I am number two, and closer to number three than
the number one."*

The more time Federer and Nadal spent together, the more
they grew genuinely to like each other. For all their surface
differences and the language barrier, they discovered plenty of
common ground: a sister who shuns the limelight, a comfortable and conventional family upbringing, fond feelings for an
understated hometown, a love of soccer, a similar sports code,
a shared sense of how a top athlete ought to comport himself.
Together they decided to take an active role in ATP politics,
turned off as they were by the CEO at the time, Etienne de
Villiers, a slick, name-dropping former Disney executive prone
to speaking in glib analogies.† (Through their surrogates, both
Nadal and Federer analogized de Villiers to the tennis player
who may have had all the shots in his arsenal but couldn't execute and make the right choices under pressure.) The com-

---

* And, of course, there was the surreal episode following the final of the 2009
Australian Open. After falling to Nadal in five sets, Federer broke down
while addressing the crowd, sobbing uncontrollably. "God, it's killing me,"
he blurted, before giving up the microphone. Nadal then approached the
stage and, before speaking, consoled Federer, the rival he had just beaten.
Wrapping a solicitous arm around him, Nadal leaned in and said, "You are a
great champion. You're going to improve on the fourteen [Grand Slam titles]
record."

† A personal favorite: "Turkeys don't get to vote for Thanksgiving."

mon values of Federer and Nadal were also validated by their mutual coolness toward Novak Djokovic, the ascending Serbian who at times seems poised to turn the Federer-Nadal rivalry into a "trivalry." Djokovic became one of the few players, if not the lone one, to trigger the umbrage of Nadal when he mimicked the Spaniard in public—down to his regrettable habit of knicker-picking. *Colleagues don't do that to each other.* Federer has taken exception to what he considers the boorishness and crassness of the Djokovic clan.

But the real epoxy in their bond was their matches. How could Nadal not respect the opulent talent of Federer? How could Federer not appreciate Nadal's athleticism and competitive will? Independently, each came to the conclusion that if the rivalry deprived him of a few titles, they would ultimately be better for it. An hour after he won the 2007 Wimbledon final, Federer told me that beating Nadal made the occasion particularly special. "In a way, I was looking for a match like this," he admitted to me later that afternoon. "Getting to a Grand Slam final, playing Nadal, five sets. It was an ultimate test, and it feels great to come through it."

Given the nature of a rivalry, there are limits to how close a friendship they can forge. Asked if he and Federer are friends, Nadal demurs: "My friends are from Majorca, the ones I went to school with when I was five years old. My English can improve, and so you know it can be tough to have a very close friend because of my English." Then: "For sure we have a good relationship. We always talk a lot."

The most enduring sports rivalries come with representations that, while often simplistic, go beyond the athletes themselves. It's the explosive passion of McEnroe juxtaposed with the tamped-down cool of Borg. (Ironically, it was Borg, the erstwhile stoic, the measured "Ice King," who would impulsively retire, dabble with women and drugs, and flirt with bankruptcy.) With Cold War echoes reverberating, it was Evert, notionally anyway, the prim and soft girl next door, pitted against Navratilova, the muscled, opinionated lesbian émigré.

The Nadal-Federer dichotomy is usually framed in a way favorable to Federer. It's artistry versus labor, the ethereal versus the earthly. A friend of mine suggests that in Europe, so many are invested in the artistry of Federer because he affirms the current times. Throughout the bloody twentieth century and the Cold War, western Europe was either engaged in conflict or fearful of it. The past twenty years marked a period of "postconflict." Culture and beauty and art could thrive and command attention and resources once devoted to something as base and basic as survival. Federer, likewise, can make art without dirtying himself. Nadal is inevitably cast as the belligerent, inelegant grinder. As one writer for *GQ* characterized it, Federer "is the sport's king and queen, thoughtful and fluent"; Nadal is "this side of beef rolling around in the clay, an ass-picking musclehead, all biceps and pantalones."

Nadal fares better when the rivalry is framed by a theme of masculinity, two opposing definitions of manliness. With his bulging muscles and abundant sweat and all that oomphing exertion, there's something undeniably macho about Nadal. Federer is rather more precious. My *Sports Illustrated* colleague S. L. Price once described Nadal as a street thug crashing a cotillion: "That he does so while oozing testosterone, flexing his biceps in a sleeveless shirt, only seals the image of a man's man, Marlon Brando to Federer's Fred Astaire." That Nadal often seems to emasculate Federer when they play — the 6–0 third set in the French Open final the most recent example — provides still more fodder.

An hour after Federer lost to Nadal in the final of the 2006 French Open, Mats Wilander, the three-time champ in Paris, sat on the terrace of the Roland Garros players' lounge shaking his head. As astute commentator and respected voice, sometimes too candid for his own good, Wilander didn't conceal his disappointment with the match: "Federer's body language was so defeatist, he took few risks, he appeared genuinely intimidated by Nadal." Then Wilander, without any trace of joking, told me, "Rafael has the one thing that Roger doesn't: balls. I don't even think Rafael has two; I think he has three." This foray into amateur anatomy was not a onetime thing either. On his own website, Wilander reconsidered the issue: "[Federer] might have them, but against Nadal they shrink to a very small size, and it's not once, it's every time."

It was a graceless choice of words. And one couldn't help but notice that Federer had won seven Grand Slams at the time, the same number Wilander had claimed. One more title and Wilander's endowment, so to speak, would be eclipsed. Still, there was something compelling about the choice of metaphor. Federer claims to read and listen to very little media chatter. But Wilander's observation wasn't a condemnation of his forehand or his propensity to serve out wide to deuce court. This was an indictment of his *manhood*. And, uncharacteristically, he fired back, telling Price, "From a former top player—almost a legend of the game—to hear stuff like this is obviously very disappointing. I thought I got along well with him; I probably still am, because he never told these things to my face. Next time I see him, maybe I'll say something. Or maybe he's not a man to be around for me. Because if you say stuff like this? There's professional [life] and there's friendship, but if you cross the line too many times eventually you're going to lose your friends. That's maybe what he's doing."

And yet, Federer being Federer, he was happy to shake Wilander's hand and offer an enthusiastic "Hi, Mats" when he saw him at various tournaments. In 2008, Wilander was working at the French Open for the Eurosport network and requested to interview Federer after a match. Federer agreed. When the conversation turned to Nadal, Wilander said, "I have to apologize for using some bad words about you a couple of years ago," smacking Federer on the shoulder, "but I did think you had a complex." Federer smiled wryly and said, "Okay," without making Wilander twist, but without exonerating him either. Then Federer went back to answering the question. Soft Power diplomacy had won out again.

Here, midway through the fourth set, Federer was showing balls. Brass ones, in fact. Four Sundays earlier in Paris, he retreated after Nadal bullied him during the first two sets. Now he was retaliating. Slowly but perceptibly he seized authority over the match, offering up his near-inexhaustible repertoire of shots. He followed a second serve to the net and blocked back a gorgeous volley. He served an ace, his one hundredth of the tournament. He worked angles like a diamond cutter until he'd opened the court and pounded a winner. All without doing anything as gauche as sweating or grunting.

When Federer held serve for 2–2, he walked to his chair and switched rackets. As so many players do, he summoned the ball boy to help yank off the cellophane wrapping, a silly ritual that makes a common plastic bag look as if it's made of some polymer so heavy it requires a second person to remove. When one first sees Federer performing one of these midset racket switches, it's easy to attribute it to a rare display of whim. Really, it's the opposite. Federer likes to change his racket at the same time the balls are replaced. (This occurs after the first seven games of play and every nine games thereafter.) Problem is, he doesn't like to serve when he uses his new racket for the first time. He had done the math in his head and determined he'd better swap sticks now or he'd be left serving with a new racket. Even in the guts of a Wimbledon final, his mind is fixed on order and organization. As Federer glided through his service games, Nadal toiled away, grunting loudly, saturated with sweat. Between points, his breathing was audible from my green bench in the media section, a half-dozen rows behind the court. With every winner, he pumped his fists in self-exhortation.

Even in repose, Nadal's physique is jarring. His arms, in particular, look like Yule logs covered with thick cables of veins. When he pumps his fists, Nadal might as well be one of those oiled competitive bodybuilders striking a pose. A generation ago, Nadal's sculpted upper body would simply have triggered admiration and inevitable comparisons to Adonis or Hercules or Popeye. His stamina would have been assumed to be the honest legacy of all the time and effort expended on the practice court.

The contemporary athlete, sadly, is not accorded this benefit of the doubt. Hypertrophied muscles? Uncommon durability? Speed records? "Youngest evers" and "oldest evers"? Excellence in general? Today they all come with a healthy side order of cynicism. "That's all well and good," says the sports chattering class, "but I need to see the clean piss test and red blood cell count before I'm totally sold."

Just days before the 2008 Wimbledon final, an American swimmer, Dara Torres, made a stirring comeback at the U.S. Olympic trials. A forty-one-year-old mother, Torres had returned from a six-year competitive absence and qualified for the Summer Games in Beijing. By conventional measures, it was a remarkable achievement. Yet the air was thick with innuendo. An ESPN on-line poll asked readers whether they suspected Torres had come by these results honestly or, it went without saying, with the help of pharmacological rocket fuel.

Absent a shred of evidence, more than one-third of the thousands of respondents suspected that she'd cheated.

The skepticism, mind you, exists for good reason. Anabolic steroids, human growth hormone, EPO (blood doping)—"performance-enhancing drugs," or PEDs, is the anodyne catchall term—are like a bad case of termites, gnawing away at the foundation of sports. And we've been burned too many times to think otherwise. In America, baseball players demolished home run records and fired 95 mph fastballs into their forties, thanks, we later learned, to "juicing" with all manner of banned substances. In Europe, for years PEDs had been common, if not altogether de rigueur, among riders in the Tour de France, stripping the event of all credibility, the winner simply assumed to be the most adept drug cheat, not the most adept cyclist. Olympic track stars and swimmers, boxers and wrestlers, even table tennis players, too numerous to catalog here, have been penalized for doping. And they're just the subset who were caught.

Worse still, even when athletes proclaim that they're clean, they might just be protesting too loudly. The baseball player Rafael Palmeiro waved a defiant finger before the U.S. Congress and asserted, "I have never used steroids, period. I don't know how to say it any more clearly than that. Never." Months later, he failed a test for the steroid stanozolol. The track star Marion Jones was so eager to deny long-standing suspicions that her Olympic gold medals were stained by doping that she used all of page 173 of her autobiography to assert, in large red letters, *I HAVE ALWAYS BEEN UNEQUIVOCAL IN MY OPINION: I AM AGAINST PERFORMANCE ENHANCING DRUGS. I HAVE NEVER TAKEN THEM AND I NEVER WILL TAKE THEM.* In 2007, she pleaded guilty to lying to federal investigators about her drug use, conceding that she had injected and applied then-undetectable steroids prior to the 2000 Sydney Olympics.*

Presumably because of his dipstick arms and the lack of bellicosity in his playing style, Federer has managed to avoid these doubts by the armchair detective. But Nadal hasn't been as lucky. His ascent, coupled with his tumescent muscles, has — sadly, unfairly — prompted a good deal of reckless speculation. During Wimbledon in 2006, a Spanish doctor had been caught with steroids, frozen blood, and transfusion apparatus during the Tour de France. One European newspaper reported that the doctor had a list of clients that included Nadal. Nadal, for the only time in memory, betrayed outright anger in public. He reacted immediately, declaring to the tennis media in an almost impenetrable accent: "People who write lies about other people are bad people."

The report, it turned out, was utterly bogus; one suspects that if Nadal had had the time or inclination, he'd have had a strong libel case. But whispers about him have persisted. Even at Wimbledon in 2008, a *Los Angeles Times* columnist, citing no evidence or named sources, but rather the suspicions of "my friend Tom, a tennis fanatic if one ever lived," openly wondered whether Nadal was succeeding "naturally."

The great sin of PEDs is that they undercut the dignity and integrity of competition. Losers win and winners lose. But the collateral damage is an ugly skepticism, the death of the simple notion that there are members of the species who are admirably superior. The "freaks," once admired for some combi-

---

* Alex Rodriguez, the Yankees star, explained to Katie Couric of CBS that he'd never used PEDs, in part because he "never felt overmatched" on the field. Barely a year later, he admitted to being another member of baseball's "Steroids Culture."

nation of their genetics, work ethic, and native talent, are now subject to question. If they remain silent, it's "What are they hiding?" If they assert their innocence, well, "Look at Marion Jones."

In regard to Nadal, the speculation is particularly sad. If tennis isn't one hundred percent clean—what industry is?—for all that ails the sport, PEDs are not high on the list. I've asked a number of players, from stars to the proletariat, to estimate what percentage of their colleagues they suspect are doping. I've yet to hear an answer in excess of "maybe a few." But never mind the absence of anecdotal evidence. In 2008, there were around 2,200 drug tests administered to 670 professional players. Of those tests, there were only 2 doping offenses, and only 1 of those was for PEDs.

The Republic of Tennis would prefer you to believe that its athletes are morally superior to those in other sports. There are two better explanations. First, tennis doesn't especially lend itself to doping. It's more a sport of hand-eye coordination, technique, and mental fitness than it is a sport of raw speed and brute strength. The sheer mass wrought from anabolics would likely do more harm than good, particularly if it came at the expense of movement and quickness. True, certain PEDs that accelerate recovery time, increase workout capacity, and boost stamina could be beneficial for tennis players, but the players still need to execute the shots. What's more, it's difficult for athletes with an eleven-month season to cycle on and off a doping regimen.

Second, and more important, tennis has one of the most rigorous and systematic anti-doping policies in all of sports. Unlike most professional leagues, which, problematically, administer tests in accordance with rules that they themselves have developed, tennis has signed on to the testing code of the

World Anti-Doping Agency (WADA), an independent body. Under the WADA code, athletes are tested in and out of competition, with no advance notice, both randomly and at anticipated times, via urine and blood, for hundreds of substances, from androstenedione to zilpaterol. Tennis players have been summoned for testing on the morning of their birthdays and on Christmas Day. Although the testing is random at tournaments, as a matter of ritual, the winners—i.e., Federer and Nadal—are forced to submit blood or urine samples. (The rationale: tennis wants to demonstrate that its champions are clean champions.) Often winners attend their postmatch press conferences wearing Band-Aids on their forearms, blood having been drawn from their veins minutes after they walked off the court.

When a player is tested, the sample is collected and sent to a WADA-accredited lab in Montreal. The results are analyzed and the sample is stored. If a new drug emerges after the test, the sample can be analyzed retroactively. HGH, for instance, was once considered undetectable, but it can now be screened for in previous samples. The WADA code also calls for transparency. Want to know how many times a player has been tested? Where, when, and for what? It's all available on the ITF's website. With a minimum of on-line sleuthing, one can discover that Nadal and Federer were each tested more than a dozen times in 2008, in and out of competition, both urine and blood. They were also tested by other agencies, like their home country's Olympic federations. And players need not fail a test to face a penalty. Possession of PEDs is a doping offense. So is declining to submit a sample to one of the collection agents who walk surreptitiously around the locker rooms at tournaments and knock on the doors of players' homes.

When you declare a contemporary athlete clean, you do so

at your own peril. But it's not just unlikely that a top tennis player's success or muscles or stamina is the product of anything other than genetics and industriousness. It's damn near impossible.

As shafts of early evening sun illuminated Centre Court, Federer and Nadal played a game of can-you-top-this? for most of the fourth set. Expelling a *YAAAaaaa* grunt, Nadal would paste a muscular forehand that recalled the old line about the baseball player Willie Mays: "The only player who could catch up to that ball, hit that ball." Federer would respond with an impeccably placed serve or, maneuvering with a sort of liquid smoothness—light on his feet, never off balance—work himself into position and finish off the point with a shot to the open court. For most players, the incoming ball eliminates possibilities; Nadal and Federer appear immune to this principle, shifting from defense to offense in a single shot.

Watching tennis up close, one realizes just how many body parts are involved in the physical act of hitting a ball. The arms get the bulk of the credit, but it's the legs that provide the thrust on the serve. It's the core—abdomen, back, and thighs—that generates the torque when a player swings. The forearm and wrist can help dispense spin. Which is why the top players in the world can have such different body types. In the ATP's top 20 alone, players' heights range from 5'5" to 6'10".

Federer leveled the fourth set, 4–4, with a pair of aggressive forehands. As Pascal Maria called out the score, Federer looked approvingly at his racket, his graphite Excalibur. When Federer was ten, his mother gave him a racket made by Wilson, a Chicago-based sporting goods company and the world's largest manufacturer of rackets. By the time he was a teenager,

Federer was sponsored by Wilson, receiving all the equipment and gear he wanted, gratis. Wilson's "beachhead investment" paid off. Federer has been with the company ever since.

Federer is paid generously to endorse Wilson — well into seven figures after performance bonuses, and he has a lifetime deal — but he could also make a credible claim to research-and-development royalties on his current racket. Several years ago, representatives from Wilson approached him about switching from his Wilson nCode to a new model. A new line of rackets means more sales to the tennis-playing public, so companies hope the stars under contract are willing to adapt to the latest technology. Some are. But equipment choice is deeply personal, and top players often take a "Why mess with success?" approach. Sampras, for instance, vowed that he would never switch from his 85-square-inch Wilson Pro Staff frame, no matter how obsolete it became. Late in his career, his small, heavy frame came to resemble the horse and buggy on the interstate. Still, he never changed.*

---

* The standard endorsement contract contains a clause whereby players must make a "best effort" to play with the latest lines. When players are unwilling to change, they often use a "paint job," the worst-kept secret in tennis. The player wants to compete with his trusty old model X. The company paying him a hefty fee wants to market model Y. In a dishonest compromise, the player competes with X but, to fool the public, dolls it up to look like Y. The paint job is the equivalent of putting a BMW 3 Series engine in the body of a 5 Series. During Wimbledon 2008, Novak Djokovic took the concept of a paint job to a new extreme. Playing the Queen's Club tune-up event, Djokovic felt that the Adidas shoes he was being paid to endorse caused him to slip on the grass courts. He took matters into his own hands — or feet — and showed up for Wimbledon wearing Nike Air Max trainers, having first obscured the swooshes and Nike lettering with white paint. When the ruse was discovered, Adidas, in a truly postmodern sports moment, released a statement explaining that the company "is committed to providing the best possible sportswear products to inspire and enable all athletes to achieve their

Antoine Ballon, Wilson's global head of marketing for per-formance rackets, asked Federer to describe what he desired in his next racket. Federer explained that he was willing to surren-der power and head size in exchange for more control. With that directive, Wilson's team of racket technologists spent the next year developing prototypes in their labs. They embedded carbon nanofibers in the graphite base, creating a racket that was relatively heavy and relatively stiff and evenly weighted, and had the same smallish, 90-square-inch head.

With a prototype finally finished, Ballon approached Federer and braced for a response. Often racket reps hand a player a model that represents millions of dollars and count-less hours of investment. Almost intuitively, the player either likes it or doesn't. Pressed to articulate their likes and dislikes, the responses are often vague. *It sucks. It feels weird. I'm not comfortable with it.* Federer, by contrast, was "incredibly, in-credibly sensitive," says Ballon. "He'd say things like, 'When I hit a backhand volley a little off center, it feels a bit too stiff.'" Wilson went back to the proverbial drawing board, and for the next year or so, Federer tested dozens of different prototypes.

Ballon also asked for Federer's input with respect to the cosmetics of the racket. Federer was okay with the red-and-white color scheme, reckoning that it mimicked Switzerland's flag. But he suggested the coloring was too bright. *Too bright?* Federer was concerned that when the ball met the racket, the

---

impossible. However, in the tradition of our founder Adi Dassler, we do not oblige athletes to wear a product in competition they do not feel are 100 percent suitable to their style of play." Djokovic released a statement of his own: "Over the past five years, Adidas' commitment to my career has been unbeatable. Adidas Tennis has actively sought my feedback on new products and technologies and I am excited to work on new products for the 2009 season."

white stripe running along its length would momentarily distract him. After sixteen different designs were proposed to Federer, he at last found one that met his approval. "That looks okay," he said coolly. "Let me show it to Mirka." She apparently liked the design. Ballon recalls that Federer returned a few minutes later and said triumphantly, "It's great! Let's do it!"

At the 2006 U.S. Open, Wilson reps again met with Federer and gave him the latest prototypes. He tested them on the practice courts. "You're going in the right direction, but you're not there yet," Ballon recalls Federer saying. The Wilson team worked through the fall, making minute adjustments to the weight and the stiffness. Finally they presented Federer with a racket that met his playing demands and aesthetic standards and came with his requested grip. The 90-inch head meant he'd still be using the smallest racket of any player on the tour, but it would provide him with additional feel. He'd settle for that tradeoff.

Federer agreed to debut what was officially called the [K] Factor [K] Six.One Tour 90 racket at the 2007 Australian Open. Wilson, however, kept the news of the racket switch under wraps. Had Federer lost in the tournament, the racket—though Federer had helped design it—would likely have been blamed, and Wilson would have taken a PR hit. As it was, Federer won the title, and Wilson's splashy marketing campaign unfolded in the forthcoming weeks.

The [K] Factor racket served Federer well for the rest of the season and was profitable for Wilson, but it came under scrutiny during his slumplet of 2008. As Federer shanked balls off the frame with increasing frequency, critics cited the small head size and noted that, especially against Nadal, whose heavily spun shots make it difficult to hit the ball squarely in the center of the racket, Federer sorely needed a larger surface area.

Yet, stubborn/loyal/professional to the end, Federer dismissed suggestions that his equipment was in any way to blame.

Not surprisingly, Nadal is decidedly less fussy about his equipment. His attitude recalls the Alan Ladd character in the movie *Shane:* "A gun is just a tool . . . as good or as bad as the man that uses it." Since his early years in the juniors, Nadal has been playing with rackets manufactured by Babolat, a French company that has been in tennis since the 1800s but has been making rackets only since the late 1990s. Carlos Moya, the Majorcan who preceded Nadal, has long played with a Babolat racket. This was all the testimonial that Nadal required.

While Nadal has switched models several times over the course of his career, Eric Babolat, the fifth-generation head of the company, describes Nadal as a "dream" player. Which is to say that (a) he wins a lot of matches, and (b) he's not picky. It's no coincidence that as Nadal has become a force, his weapon of choice, Babolat's AeroPro Drive model, has become the best-selling racket in Europe. And Nadal is not exactly hung up on the minutiae. Toni Nadal laughingly recalls Rafael's once playing with a set of rackets that looked different from one another. To satisfy his curiosity, Toni weighed them, and he discovered that some were as much as 30 grams heavier — a variation of roughly ten percent — than others. Yet his nephew had never perceived the difference.

Nadal's racket is painted canary yellow and is manufactured in China. Even with a bit of weighting on the perimeter that makes the head heavier than the body — the one minor bit of customization that separates Nadal's racket from the one you and I can buy in the store for a list price of $185, unstrung — the racket weighs only 312 grams. (Federer's racket weighs closer to 400 grams.) Nadal's head size is 100 square inches.

The one strikingly unusual feature of Nadal's racket is the

grip size. Though Nadal's hands are by no means small, his grip is just 4⅛ inches, the handle circumference of many junior rackets. Most ATP pros use grips of at least 4½ inches. While Federer's grip is 4⅜, he usually applies several layers of overgrip. Sampras, whose hands are no bigger than Nadal's, had a grip exceeding 5 inches. Nadal insists that the small grip enables him to wrap his hands around the base and use more wrist to generate his blindingly fast racket head acceleration, and thus his power. (It may also explain his iffy net game: that lollipop stick of a grip robs him of some feel on his volley, especially when he doesn't hit the ball right in the middle of the racket.) In short, Federer's and Nadal's rackets are as different as the players wielding them.

When critics—John McEnroe chief among them—complain that the lighter and wider rackets encourage overhitting and play a major role in bleaching artistry from the sport, they tend to overstate the impact of technology. Racket manufacturers trumpet their "revolutionary" products, but in truth most contemporary models are only marginally more powerful than their wooden forebears. And contrary to conventional thinking, the rackets have not given an unfair advantage to the server and the heavy hitters; they've helped the smaller players who, though once consigned by their physical limitations to play defensive chess, can whale away. Ivo Karlovic, the gangly, six-foot-ten Croatian, may be an inartistic ace machine, but he can hit the hell out of the ball with any handled implement this side of a frying pan. Give Nadal a wooden racket, however, and he would probably be forced to block back serves rather than return them with big cuts. He would be playing defensive slices instead of whipping his lasers. If the new rackets have eliminated "classic" tennis and serve-and-volleying, there's a corollary: they have diversified the field.

And it has ever been thus in tennis. As one prominent

player griped: "Once the first flush of youth and athletic prowess starts to fade, the modern game disintegrates because it has no solid and intelligent foundation on which to depend. Speed and power are essential in the equipment of every great player, but they alone cannot suffice." That was Bill Tilden, speaking in 1950.

A more significant, if less heralded, agent of change has been the strings. For decades, top players slugged the ball with strings made of natural gut—derived from the innards of cows, not cats, as is often misstated—or synthetic gut that had similar properties. The players strung their rackets at high tension. Bjorn Borg, for example, was known to string his rackets at such extreme tension that he was sometimes woken up in the middle of the night by the sound of his strings snapping.

Several years ago, string companies—most notably a Belgian company, Luxilon—began to develop and market a synthetic, polyester-based string. The move from gut string to polyester has revolutionized the sport every bit as much as the move from wood to graphite rackets. The first time Andre Agassi used Luxilon, he jokingly declared that it should be illegal. "I can't miss!" he said.

That was in 2002. Today virtually every pro uses polyester string. Nadal uses Babolat's thick polyester string. Roman Prokes, a prominent stringer to the stars, suspects that "if Nadal swings the way he does with gut strings, he wouldn't hit a single ball in the court." Federer uses a hybrid of natural gut on the "mains," or vertical axis, and polyester on the "cross," or horizontal axis. Polyester string doesn't snap easily, but it loses its tension quickly, so for a match Federer and Nadal will arm themselves with as many as a dozen rackets.

Ask twelve experts to explain the physics of polyester-based string—in short, what makes it so damn magical—and you get at least a dozen answers. Pros liken polyester string to having "no shock absorber" on the racket. The thick, inelastic string grips and holds the ball on the racket face. A former Grand Slam champion compares Luxilon to having "suction cups on your racket" that enable the ball to stay on the string a millisecond longer, supposedly generating spin in the process. Yet a well-regarded guru gives an opposite explanation, positing that polyester string is low friction and, unlike gut, quickly snaps back into place after contact, causing the ball to pop off the racket face. Go figure.

Using physics to explain the benefits of polyester-based string is a dodgy proposition. There's been very little definitive testing or data, and the companies aren't rushing to disseminate their secret. One suspects that the real benefit of polyester string is psychological. It has become a self-fulfilling prophecy. A player's swing speed is determined less by the weight of the racket than by a *perception* of whether he'll miss. Tell players that the string in their rackets will empower them to pummel the ball and it will stay in the court, and they'll swing away fearlessly. And so they do.

Commentators and armchair critics like to spout off about the effects of technology, yet it can have the effect of trivializing the athletes. In any sport, compare today's players with their ancestors: they are taller, more muscular, and more flexible. It's abundantly clear that they train harder and smarter, eat better, and have the benefit of more scientific information. They learned advanced techniques at an earlier age, and—because more people from more countries are playing the sport—they face stronger competition. As the sport grows and becomes more capitalized, academies and federations and even marginal pro players can afford personal trainers and nutritionists and other specialists. Ultimately, this pushes the sport forward far more than advances in equipment.

• • •

David Law was stationed high above Centre Court, alone in a commentary box roughly the size of an airplane lavatory. Law was working for BBC Radio's 5 Live, tasked with articulating statistical trends. For the first three sets, Law would get some airtime every few games and hold forth on Federer's second-serve percentage or Nadal's failure to serve-and-volley or Nadal's decision to serve into Federer's body twenty-five percent of the time. When he wasn't noting such trends, Law found himself broadcasting the match to himself: "No! . . . Not possible! . . . The quality will not dip!"

By the fourth set, Law began to feel conflicted about his BBC work. When the producer called up to the booth for the next statistical report, Law demurred. "Statistics are irrelevant now," he said. "This is not something that numbers can describe. If you take one second away from describing the action and the atmosphere, it'll be a second wasted." The producer got a similar message from Michael Stich. The 1991 Wimbledon champ had been broadcasting the match for BBC Radio, but he was ready to walk out of the studio. "I want to go into the crowd and start yelling!" he exclaimed. "I'm working for you, but I want to be a fan!"

Serving at 5–6 to stay in the match/tournament/tennis hierarchy, Federer played a clinical, efficient game. Relying on muscle memory, depriving himself of the opportunity even to consider the stakes, he pounded away at his serve and forehand, forcing still another tiebreaker. It was Virginia Wade, the last Brit to win Wimbledon, who once described Centre Court as having the personality of both an august grandmother and an exuberant teenager. Here was a vivid illustration. Swiveling their heads in unison as they followed the ball, the fans watched points in dead quiet, the acoustics limited to the sounds of racket hitting ball, shoes squeaking on grass, and Nadal's *eeeaaaaaHHHH-UUUUGGGGhhhhhh* grunting.

As soon as the point ended, Centre Court came to rival any sports coliseum filled with apoplectic partisans held in thrall. The competing cheers of "Roger!" and "Rafa!" mixed with rhythmic foot-stomping formed a sort of cacophonous symphony.

Somehow, the level of the tennis and the drama managed to spike during the tiebreaker. On the first point, Nadal made a rare escape from the baseline and punched a superb forehand volley, simultaneously showing off his improved confidence and improved aptitude at the net. Federer uncorked a parabolic topspin lob, remembering to reverse his thinking and direct the ball to Nadal's right side. With his back to the net, Nadal reached into the air and flicked a backhand overhead—perhaps the single most difficult shot in tennis. He could scarcely have executed the shot better, cutting the ball at an extreme angle. Federer anticipated it, though, caught up to the ball, and thwacked a forehand past Nadal. Those watching on television were deprived of the full effect, as exulting fans jumped in front of the baseline camera with arms raised.

Unflustered, Nadal won the next point with a blistering forehand and then induced another error from Federer's backhand. There had been no break points for the entire set, yet the first three points of the tiebreaker had gone to the returner. While Nadal battled pugnaciously, winning point after point and showing no emotion, Federer muttered to himself with each lost opportunity. At 5–2, Nadal had a chance to serve out the match and win the Wimbledon title.

And he blinked.

It was as if his inoculation against the pressure had worn off. Though Nadal would later deny it, it's difficult to believe that, at least in some small recess of his brain, he wasn't already picturing himself as champion. He claims he'd never been more nervous in his life, scarcely able to grip his racket.

In the poised silence, he missed a first serve, eliciting an "Awww" from the nervous crowd. In the box, Toni nudged Carlos Costa, the agent: "Rafa's going to double-fault." Sure enough, Nadal's second offering skidded shakily off the net, a terrifically ill-timed double fault. "You were right," Costa whispered to Toni. Nadal smiled gamely, but at 5–3, he missed a routine forehand into the net, and this time he reacted, glaring at the net as if to say, "What the hell are *you* doing here?" He then pantomimed throwing his racket, his first show of truly negative emotion all day.

Gifted two points, Federer, now serving at 4–5, took full advantage, punishing a forehand winner and then clocking an unreturnable serve. Ninety seconds earlier, Nadal had been serving for the Wimbledon title. Now Federer was one point from the fourth set. A fickle beast, momentum. When Pascal Maria called the score — "Six, five. Federer." — he had to strain to be heard over the crowd. "What could you do?" Nadal later recalled thinking. "You just had to keep fighting." So he did, winning an eighteen-stroke rally when Federer missed a forehand and then securing a match point when Federer missed another forehand, the error confirmed by replay.

Without giving himself a chance to contemplate the "what ifs" of losing the next point, Federer quickly went into his service motion, his mind as close to vacant as possible. His serve drilled the corner of the box and the ball dribbled innocuously off Nadal's racket. It was 7–7 and the crowd exhaled en masse: *At least this next point won't decide the title.* But the emotional breather was short-lived.

Federer painted the corner of the court with a forehand. Stationed maybe fifteen feet behind the baseline, Nadal scrambled and, on the dead run, with his left arm extended, flung a whipping, dipping forehand up the line. Federer let out a rare yell — "A howl of anguish," the BBC termed it — as he lunged for the ball. But it zipped by him and, saturated with topspin, dive-bombed into the court. Again the raised arms of the exuberant fans obscured the television cameras. Nadal sank to both knees and performed a congratulatory double fist-pump. He immediately popped up, aware that he was still obligated to win an additional point. Nadal's father, Sebastian, his smart pinstripe suit starting to ruffle, buried his head in his hands, overcome by it all.

Then it was Federer's turn for genius. After thwarting Federer with a tricky serve out wide, Nadal smacked a forehand that pinned Federer behind the baseline and prodded him off the court behind the doubles alley. Plus, the ball was coming to Federer's weaker, backhand side, somersaulting with spin. Quick parlor game: One point from the title, Nadal can pick a one-two combination to win Wimbledon. What should it be? Answer: It's hard to imagine him choosing anything other than a wide serve and then a short forehand approach to Federer's backhand.

Anything less than a perfect shot, and the match—the tournament, the reign of supremacy—was over. Federer reared back and bent low to the grass. Forestalling future debate about his reserves of courage, he blistered a backhand up the line. Nadal, like any good rival, had forced Federer to plumb new dimensions of his character and his game. And this is what he came up with. By the time Nadal reacted, the ball had passed him and landed well within the lines. Federer didn't merely pull off an exceptionally difficult shot under immense pressure; he made it look uncomplicated. Once again the fans—those allegedly reserved, prissy tennis fans—raised their arms and blocked the cameraman. In the NBC booth, John McEnroe, normally so glib, struggled to locate the words. "It's only fitting, isn't it?" was all he finally managed to say.

Even Sebastian Nadal, having just watched his son fail to

convert match point, reflexively applauded the brilliance. In the players' box, other members of Team Nadal and Team Federer exchanged warm looks of disbelief. Arguably the two best shots of the tournament had been hit on successive points. After the applause died down, Pascal Maria leaned into his microphone. Unable to suppress his enjoyment, he appeared to giggle slightly as he said, "Eight all."

Catalyzed, Federer won the next point with a penetrating forehand. Holding set point, he missed a first serve and then gently guided his second offering into the box. When Nadal's return landed beyond the baseline, the tiebreaker, a fourteen-minute, eighteen-point passion play, was over. 7–6. Federer yelled "Yeeahhh!" and performed a happy 360-degree pirouette. Nadal walked off the court solemnly, and his uncle shook his head and looked downward. The volume of the crowd approximated that of a rock concert. Nadal and Federer had now played 302 points. Each had won 151. It was 7:30 in the evening, and the 2008 Wimbledon final was headed to a fifth set.

Of course it was.

Fifth Set

9–7

THE FIFTEEN THOUSAND FANS fortunate enough to have scored Centre Court tickets made up just a minuscule fraction of the match's audience. Television is the lifeblood of most sports, and tennis is no exception. The 2008 Wimbledon final was shown by 85 networks in 185 countries, with a reach of billions. The various networks paid rights fees to the All England Club, the amount varying in accordance with the size of the potential market. While the club doesn't release figures, suffice it to say that NBC, which holds exclusive rights to air the final live in the United States, paid more — purportedly in excess of $10 million — than, say, Poland's Polsat network. When Steffi Graf and Boris Becker were winning Wimbledon titles as a matter of course, rights in Germany went for far more than they do today. On the other hand, thanks to Nadal, the rights fees charged to Spanish broadcasters are now far more costly than, say, five years ago.

The largest networks are assigned claustrophobically small broadcast booths at Centre Court, but the real hive of activity is fifty or so yards away at the multistory television compound. If the players' area at Wimbledon resembles a cruise ship, the adjacent television compound might be compared to a hospital. The various rights-holding networks are each assigned a suite, the size commensurate with the scale of the operation. There are triage rooms and trauma rooms and frantic workers barging through swinging doors. Jamie Reynolds, who oversees ESPN's broadcast, takes the hospital analogy further: "If the screen goes blank, it's a bad thing."

True to form, Wimbledon has a unique television policy. The matches are televised domestically on BBC and BBC 1, the British terrestrial network that all citizens subsidize, whether they like it or not. In exchange for transmission rights, the BBC also agrees to be the "host broadcaster" for the event, paying for continuous coverage of the seven courts for the two weeks. The forty BBC cameras scattered throughout the grounds — nine are on Centre Court — feed images to a main control center. (NBC, the only network granted an exception, is permitted three of its own cameras on Centre Court.)

In the television compound, producers and directors from the other rights-holding networks take the BBC feeds. As if given a bowl of plain lettuce at the salad bar, they are then free to garnish and enhance the feeds as they please, choosing which matches they want to air and adding graphics or statistics or so-called punctuation points. ESPN, for instance, imports a staff of 125 employees to embellish the feeds. (For smaller countries — say, New Zealand — there is a cheaper option. They pay for a composite "world feed," a complete program created by the in-house Wimbledon production company. Think of this as television's answer to a newspaper wire story.)

Though the various networks get the same basic feed, the differences in broadcast philosophies among the networks are vast. Mimicking American television dramas that seldom linger on a scene for more than ninety seconds, the ESPN coverage often ricochets from court to court. It's what Reynolds calls "a golf approach, a full-fan experience." By contrast, the Japanese broadcaster NHK dedicates its entire coverage to Japanese players, no matter what. Federer could be deadlocked in the fifth set, bleeding from the head and on fire; if, say, the Japanese player Ai Sugiyama was in action simultaneously, the broadcast would stay with her match.

As different as the various global broadcast styles might be, on the final Sunday they had this in common: as the match unfolded and evolved into a classic, there was less and less talking. In the television compound, producers issued fewer instructions. In the Centre Court broadcast booths, commentators let long measures elapse without saying a word. John McEnroe, not generally known — or, for that matter, *hired* — for his restraint, sometimes spoke so seldom that viewers could be forgiven for checking to see whether they'd inadvertently activated the mute button. As McEnroe would later recall, "Nadal and Federer were so eloquent out there with their tennis, I mean, what were any of us going to add?"

The hypothetical "best tennis match" that ESPN writer Bill Simmons had envisioned? It was happening, three weeks after his column was written. And he watched, transfixed.* Not that he was alone. In Mumbai, India, Priscilla Singh, self-described as "Federer's biggest fan," stayed up through the night, at one point stuffing a T-shirt in her mouth so her muffled screams wouldn't wake up her neighbors. In northern California, the San Francisco Giants were preparing to play the Los

---

* To his eternal credit, Simmons did repent for his column. A few days after the Wimbledon final, he interviewed James Blake on his radio show and began by joking, "So, I read this column a few weeks ago by this idiot at ESPN and he was saying that he was worried about the future of tennis. And his big premise was if someone told you that the greatest match ever was about to be played, would you even watch it? Fast-forward a few weeks later and the Greatest Match Ever was played and more than a few people watched it."

Angeles Dodgers, wrapping up a weekend baseball series. In both clubhouses, players crowded around the flat-screens, enthralled by the match. One sensed that few knew much about the sport—"Why the hell is the court green?" one player asked—but they were sucked in by the drama and had quickly picked sides, the Dominican and Latino players mostly cheering for Nadal, the Americans tending to side with Federer. On the stadium concourse, the televisions were tuned not to the baseball game but to Wimbledon, and fans gathered around to watch the conclusion of the match. Baseball could wait. This was *history.*

In Austin, Texas, Andy Roddick got off an airplane and saw that his phone was exploding with text messages. In one form or another they all asked the same question: "Can u believe this match?!" Roddick, a Wimbledon finalist a few years before, parked himself in front of a TV and watched the last set inside the airport. In Memphis, Diane Morales, the tennis sorceress, still convinced that she had been jinxing Nadal, kept her television off, though she was among the hundreds of members celebrating and commiserating on the cheering thread of vamosbrigade.com. In the French village of Naves, Peter Carry, a debonair New Yorker (full disclosure: a former boss of mine), and his wife were at their château entertaining friends. The two couples hadn't seen each other in more than a decade and had looked forward to hiking or biking in the Ardèche region. They ended up reconnecting over Wimbledon, spending most of a gorgeous summer day indoors in front of the television. As afternoon bled into evening, they postponed their dinner reservations three times.

The NBC broadcast in the United States scored a 4.6 rating, representing 5.2 million viewers, a forty-three percent increase over the previous year's final. In Great Britain, the BBC viewership peaked at 13.1 million, more than twice the viewership of the British Grand Prix auto race, which was won by a Brit, Lewis Hamilton. The match attracted 1.12 million viewers in Switzerland, more than double the previous high, Federer's 2003 final, which drew 545,000 viewers. In Spain, viewership peaked at 7 million, this in a country with a population of 40 million. In France, 2.3 million households, a huge audience, watched. For all the flaws that make tennis unappealing to television executives — the imprecise duration of matches, the diverse global audience scattered across time zones, the dead time between points — this was compulsively watchable programming. All of those casual fans who'd abandoned the sport, for whatever reason, had come screaming back. The next morning, the match would be *the* conversation around office cubicles and dinner tables, featured on the front page of the *New York Times,* and the lead segment of the national newscasts. For a few days, anyway, tennis would be king.

As if Federer needed another advantage, he would be serving to start the final set. More than two sets and four hours, including the rain delay, had elapsed since the last break of serve. Assuming the trend continued, after nine games Nadal would be saddled with the immense pressure of needing to hold his serve simply to stay in the match. A few wayward shots on his service game and he would lose. (Borg, it was noted, had the good fortune of serving first in the fifth set of the epochal 1980 final that, not coincidentally, he won.)

Bouncing on the balls of his feet, his brown eyes wide open, Federer inaugurated the fifth set by strumming a serve into Nadal's body. He served at a clipped pace — no reason to change the tempo now — and played almost fancifully. Some of his conjurings worked (a gem of an angled backhand volley) and some didn't (an ill-conceived drop shot), but his play bespoke looseness and self-belief.

In Nadal's row of the players' box, Uncle Toni dropped his head and chewed on his lip, looking like one of those crestfallen Kentucky Derby trainers whose horse got nipped at the finish line. His thoughts ricocheted. He recalled the Euro '96 soccer tournament held at Wembley Stadium, not far from the All England Club. His brother Miguel Angel had missed a kick on the penalty shootout that had enabled England to beat Spain. *Maybe the Nadals are cursed in this country,* Toni thought. He also remembered how, after the 2007 final, he walked into the locker room to see Rafa slouched in front of his locker, crying. "Don't cry," Toni said sternly. "Crying because you don't win Wimbledon? It's like if I cry because I don't have a Rolls-Royce." But that was last year. Now, to lose three straight Wimbledon finals? To the same guy each time? When you held a match point? "Then," he later said, only half jokingly, "you might be right to cry."

To Toni it all illustrated a cosmic truth in life: gain and loss are not symmetrical. To him, every action does not have an equal and opposite reaction. "Victory does not feel so good as losing feels bad," he says. "When you have a son, you are happy. But it's no comparison to the sadness you feel losing a son. When you earn one million dollars, you are happy. But when you lose one million dollars, it hurts more. If Rafa wins Wimbledon, he's happy, we're all happy. But what if he loses?" At one point, Sebastian Nadal, sitting across the aisle, shuffled over and interrupted Toni's reverie, telling his brother to do a better job camouflaging his emotions. *Rafa needs you to be positive!*

Subtly taking back some authority—unintentionally, he would later contend—Nadal slowed the pace of his service game. He bounced . . . bounced . . . bounced the ball ten, sometimes twelve, times before going into his motion. He toweled his body copiously. He inspected the balls with painstaking precision before making his selection. Asked what was going through his mind at this critical juncture starting the fifth set, Nadal had the ultimate Zen archer's response: "Nothing." No conflicting thoughts, no self-interrogation, no brain-voice suggesting he'd messed up. He was, as they say, in the moment, simply relying on the muscle memory that had been ingrained in his subconscious. He returned to the business of rocketing spin-heavy forehands and retrieving Federer's offerings — in tennis, too, the sports axiom holds: defense wins championships — and held serve with relative ease. Somehow he'd been able to compartmentalize the inconvenient truth that, moments earlier, he had blown match points. He was back to playing effective tennis. This was the emotional equivalent of the cartoon character getting knocked silly with an Acme anvil or a frying pan and recovering as if the colossal blown opportunity were a mere annoyance.

Federer resumed his breakneck pace. He served and then stormed the net. No, he said through his actions, Nadal's whistling passing shots would have no chilling effect on his aggression. He continued his varied serving. And then it was Nadal's turn to slow the tempo and grind out methodical points. It was like two siblings fighting for control of the stereo, imposing their different tastes on each other. By 2–2, the fans went from swiveling their heads horizontally to swiveling their heads vertically. Already an unsightly shade of gray, the sky began to leak rain. When the game went to deuce after Federer missed what the BBC called "a cheeky little lob," Federer, displaying his desire for order, shot Pascal Maria a displeased stare, lobbying wordlessly for play to be suspended. When the sprinkle turned to a full-on shower, Maria agreed. The players hustled off the court, and the grounds crew commenced their elaborate tarp drill for the second time of the afternoon.

If the first rain delay had served as a welcome intermission from all the intensity, the second elicited groans all around. Postponing the match now seemed akin to the film projector blowing a fuse right before the movie's final scene. Never mind the logistical complications for the television networks and fans; it would feel so wrong, so anti-climactic, to finish such an episodic match the following morning. It was somehow fitting that the last match ever to be played on a roofless Centre Court might be marred by rain.

Retreating through the foyer and to the locker room, Federer led the way, bounding up the stairs, skipping every other step. Nadal trudged behind, skipping no steps. One club employee stationed near the locker room noticed that Nadal was jogging lightly in place and suspected it was to send a message to Federer that his spirits hadn't been diminished after all. Nadal gave himself a pep talk. "I'm thinking, 'Keep it up. You're in the final. You're playing well.' If I lose, I'm going to shake his hand and say, 'Congratulations, Roger.' But I was ready to go back to work."

Uncle Toni and Maymo headed to the locker room, decidedly less exuberant than they'd been the last time they'd entered. All too aware that their man had squandered two match points to win his first Wimbledon, they expected to see him in a state of distress. To their pleasant surprise, Nadal was seated on the bench in front of his locker looking earnest but hardly downbeat.

Nadal maneuvered so that Maymo could administer a quick rubdown and apply white tape to the callused fingers on Nadal's left hand. Federer walked in and out of the locker room. If there was no physical divide between the players, the language barrier helped to provide some privacy. Federer could speak in Swiss German to Severin Lüthi, his confidant and the Swiss Davis Cup captain, just as Nadal could confer with his team in Spanish without risk of interception. Federer spent most of the time alone, in the privacy of his own thoughts.

Nadal turned to his uncle. "Try not to fall asleep this time, okay?"

Toni smiled. "I liked the position you were in a lot better the last time I was in here," he said, referring to the previous rain delay.

Nadal smiled back and shook his head. *No shit.*

Toni then turned serious and launched into a soliloquy. "Look, Rafa. Roger is going to be as nervous as you are. Right up until now, he's been playing not to lose. Now he is going to have to play to win, so he's going to be as nervous as you are. You have to hold the pressure and work with the pressure because this is your big chance to win Wimbledon. If Federer beats you, fine. But you shouldn't be the one losing. Do the right things, and don't lose confidence if you make errors."

Nadal sat and listened. When his uncle had finished, the player spoke, not boastfully, just matter-of-factly. "You know how last year, when I lost, I said I don't know if I'm ever going to be in the final again?"

"Yes," Toni said.

"Well, I know I told you that, but here I am in the final and it's not going to happen. I'm going to make it. And if I don't make it because I lose in the end, I will make it the next year. Stay calm."

Toni looked up. "You're telling me to stay calm?"

"Stay calm. I lost the two tiebreakers but he didn't break my serve in either set. I won the first and second sets, no? Why can't I win the fifth set too?"

When Maymo and Toni returned to the box, the entourage crowded in, eager to hear how their man was doing. *How's*

Rafa? How are his spirits? Toni shook his head. "Either he's the best actor alive, making great theater, or he's actually very relaxed."

In the pressroom, the media scrambled to rewrite earlier stories that had heralded a Nadal blowout. With space left aside for the final twist and the winner, the typical story contained flowery passages about what an epic match this had been. Journalists scrambled, too, to place the match in historical context. It had been 81 years — Henri Cochet over Jean Borotra — since a player had rallied from being down two sets. It had been 60 years since a player — poor Bob Falkenburg — had held match point and lost. It had been more than 120 years since Willie Renshaw won six straight Wimbledon titles, a bit misleading, since in the 1880s, the defending champion was automatically given a spot in the final.

It was also during this rain delay that the chorus grew louder: this was the Greatest Tennis Match Ever Played. It was, of course, a subjective determination, one that would surely benefit from some detachment. But really, what could top this? Two rivals meeting for the third straight Wimbledon final, playing at an unparalleled level for five sets. Assume that the Greatest Match has to be a match of gravitas — that is, it will never occur at the Memphis Open or the Budapest Classic or in an early round — and the applicant pool dwindles. The one other conceivable candidate was, of course, the McEnroe-Borg 1980 Wimbledon final. That match may have rivaled Federer-Nadal 2008 for drama, but (blasphemy alert) it didn't come close to matching this level of qualitative excellence. Spark up a videotape of that match and, even accounting for advances in technology, comparing the depth and accuracy with Federer-Nadal is really no comparison at all. Besides, the first set of that match ended with the unseemly score of 6–1 (a "breadstick," in tennis jargon), whereas every set of Federer-

Nadal 2008 had been hotly contested. Insofar as there were any lapses, they lasted for only a few points. McEnroe himself was first in line to pronounce the 2008 Wimbledon final as "the greatest match I've seen." Borg echoed this view shortly thereafter.

Tick off the Classic Sporting Event checklist and this match had it all—skill, courage, sportsmanship, grace, discipline, gallantry, poise, intelligence, humility, injury, recovery, fibrillations of momentum, even acts of God. The match was also significant for what it lacked—melodrama, pornographic trash talk, cheating. There was neither a scoreboard telling fans when to clap nor a public-address announcer with a cartoonishly baritone voice. No cheerleaders, no goofy mascots, no booing, no piped-in music during breaks in play or unnaturally peppy men firing free T-shirts into the crowd via air cannon. The moral might be this: invest some dignity in a sporting event and everyone responds in kind.

Convinced that the rain would continue and the match would require completion in the morning, television executives made contingency plans for the Monday broadcast. Fans inquired about the ticketing policy. International visitors called airlines and travel agents, investigating the possibility of rebooking flights and hotels. But fortunately, as if by pure divine intervention, this rain delay was a brief one, just half an hour. This time, Federer and Nadal made no eye contact as they returned to the court and warmed up for three minutes as the crowd filed back in. Needing no time to ease himself back into the match, Federer ran out the game with a pair of aces. 3–2.

As many times as the Republic of Tennis had seen Federer perform, it had never seen him perform quite like this. This was Federer as *fighter*. It had always been clear that Federer enjoyed playing and winning and entertaining the crowds. Recalling that John McEnroe once said that, at the height of his powers, he didn't find tennis enjoyable, I once asked Federer if he truly liked the game. "Like tennis?" he said in a tone that suggested *are you kidding?* "I love it!" But for all of Federer's relentless winning, it never appeared as if he'd cultivated a taste for battle. There are players who like nothing more than being locked in combat, fighting deep in a fifth set. Nadal, for his part, characterizes tennis as a "hobby-job" and readily admits that he enjoys the competition more than the tennis itself. Federer would rather unleash his sorcery and win 6–2, 6–2, 6–2. The back alley is not Federer's choice milieu. He'd rather soar than rumble.

This is in no way a knock on Federer, but most athletes of his stature—Woods, Jordan, Tom Brady, Roger Clemens, Sampras, the Williams sisters—manage to supplement their physical gifts with the highest levels of competitive resolve. They are "killers" and "assassins" and "snipers" when they play. That Federer is decidedly not an assassin, you could argue, only elevates his achievements. Without the overlay of mental toughness, we see just how prodigious his physical gifts are. He wins not because of any "samurai mindset" or "killer mentality." He wins because of his genius. But I have often felt hard-pressed to name an athlete with a wider disparity between talent and mental toughness.

Yet here Federer was, in the core of the fifth set of the Wimbledon final against his nemesis, and damn if he wasn't relishing the competition. Presented with a fight-or-flight option four Sundays earlier in Paris, Federer had chosen the latter and lost passively. Not so on this day. He was unquestionably fighting, patiently gaining the advantage in rallies and then slinging winners, akin to a boxer softening his opponent with jabs before unloading the straight right. He was pumping his fists and barking many a self-exhorting "Come on!," prideful and territorial as he paced around the court. His eyes were wide with intensity, as if he'd somehow forgotten how to blink. The fighting instincts that had seldom been in evidence in the past—hell, they usually didn't need to be—were now on full public display.

Trailing 3–4, 30–30, and serving, Nadal spun in a high-kicking second serve that Federer struggled to return. Nadal, though, played an oddly tentative point. On the third ball, Federer popped a forehand beyond Nadal's reach to set up break point. One more point and Federer would serve for the championship, leading 5–3. By the time the ball boy fetched the ball, the Betfair exchange was going berserk. Nadal was suddenly matching at 3.8, and Federer was trading at as low as 1.35 on the same point. In other words, had you bet $1 on Federer to win the match at this precise time, it would have paid only $1.35. The same dollar wagered on Nadal to win the match would have yielded $3.80.

Within seconds, the "stock exchange" rebounded. Nadal evened the game to deuce by pushing Federer to the corner of the court and striking his forehand with viciousness. (Did anyone really expect Nadal to play cautiously now?) Federer slapped at the ball, squash-shot style, and popped up a lazy lob. Nadal closed in, pounding an overhead so severely that, after bouncing on the court, the ball landed in the stands. Federer had now managed to capitalize on just one of the thirteen break points he had earned in the match. Nadal then used unrelenting depth to induce an error and close out the game with still another cutting forehand. 4–4. Of the 354 points that had been played, Federer had won 177 and Nadal had won 177.

Federer won his service game with ease. 5–4. The crowd spent the entire changeover chanting the players' names. Nadal now needed to hold his serve to stay in the match. And with no tiebreaker played in the fifth set, it would be thus, unless or until he could break Federer. Alternating between "*Si!*" and "Come on!" when he won points, Nadal held serve. 5–5.

They had been playing for four hours and seventeen minutes, surpassing the 1982 McEnroe-Connors encounter as the longest final in Wimbledon history. Neither Federer nor Nadal, though, exhibited the slightest outward sign of fatigue or physical withering, rare for a sporting event, much less one of this duration. No dead legs, no doubling over after long points, no heaving chests. They continued to chase every ball. The rain delays had obviously helped them conserve and replenish their rations of energy. But beyond that, both athletes were in supreme physical condition and regarded as the fittest in the sport. Their methods of training might differ, but Federer and Nadal operate on a simple principle: tennis is mostly an anaerobic sport, and training exercises should be anaerobic as well. Instead of distance running—an aerobic activity that replicates neither the mechanics nor the neuromuscular functions of tennis—the two spend more time lunging and sprinting and squatting, enduring drills that simulate the bursts of explosive movements and changes of direction that occur during a match.

Nadal is known for his stamina, but in Federer's case it's the most underrated component of his game. At the onset of his pro career, after Federer had mastered technique, he had the good sense to recognize the importance of fitness. You could have all the shots, but if you're too tired to get to the ball, what does it matter? He hired Pierre Paganini, an old coach of his from the Swiss federation, as a trainer. Several times a year, in the scorching heat of Dubai, Paganini puts Federer through the equivalent of training camp. Federer will spend four hours a day on the court, training and hitting against sparring partners that rotate in and out. Jesse Levine, a young American

pro—and, as a lefty, able to stand in for Nadal—has practiced with Federer in Dubai on numerous occasions. Levine
claims Federer often wears a heart monitor, checking his rest-
ing heart rate and recovery time. "And I still don't think I saw
Roger sweat," he cracks. One legacy of this off-court work: the
2008 Wimbledon final marked the 737th professional match
of Federer's career. Not once had he been physically unable to
finish a match.

Like the path of the ball, the momentum of the match continued to drift back and forth from one side of the net to the
other. At 5–5, Nadal afforded himself a pair of break points.
Federer calmly staved off one with his twenty-fourth ace of the
match. He saved the other with a patient, well-organized point
that he finished off with a slapping forehand. In his box, Mirka
cupped her hands and yelled instruction. Lynette Federer
clapped. "Come on, Roger," she said, in a voice audible to no
one but herself. Robert Federer, his head buried under a red
ballcap bearing his son's initials, smiled faintly, looking less intense than the fans who had not sired one of the players on the
court. Sustaining his aggression, Federer closed out the game
with a round of flawlessly struck forehands. 6–5. Again, Nadal
would have to serve to stay in the match.

It was now approaching 9 P.M. local time, "Breakfast at
Wimbledon" trespassing into the afternoon, even in California.
During the changeover, the phone in the umpire's chair began
vibrating. Maria picked up the line and his face went slack. It
was the Hawk-Eye booth calling. Because of the darkness, the
cameras were no longer able to pick up reliable images of the
ball as it landed on the court. There would be no instant replay
for the rest of the match. After turning off his microphone,
Maria quietly conveyed this to Nadal and Federer. Then he
sighed. "It had been the match of a lifetime," as he later put

it, and from an officiating standpoint it had gone well. Now, in diminishing visibility, when every point would be critical, there would not be the safety net of instant replay. He glanced over to his wife for support. Much like the players, he tried to motivate himself. "Just don't lose focus," he told himself.

Both players spent the next two games firing shots of almost ruthless accuracy. Thankfully, though, no controversial calls necessitated a replay. Nadal held his serve. 6–6. Federer then served his way out of trouble, including a 128 mph blast, equaling his second-fastest serve of the match. 7–6.

Nadal countered, opening a quick lead in his service game. At 40–15, he sprinted to the net to return a drop shot and slugged it forward. Federer took the ball out of the air at midcourt, low, and hit a swinging one-handed backhand crosscourt passing shot, an exceptionally difficult maneuver. When Federer won his first Wimbledon five years earlier, he executed virtually the same shot against Mark Philippoussis in the final, and it was held up as proof of his genius and artistry. Now he was required to hit shots like this to just stay in a game and a match.

Serving at 40–30, Nadal opened the court with a rifled forehand. Still light on his feet, Federer caught up to the ball and slapped it back over the net. After Nadal set himself up for an overhead, Federer didn't concede the point but anticipated correctly and stuck out his racket. Good fortune favoring the brave, Federer blocked back the most defensive of lobs that seemed to kiss the gray sky, but the ball landed a few inches inside Nadal's baseline, provoking shrieks from the crowd.

It was immensely frustrating for Nadal to have this easy putaway shot, only to let his opponent back into the point. But Nadal backtracked, positioned himself, and swatted the ball back in the court. On his next shot, he reared back and blasted a forehand that cut through the air and passed Federer. Sebastian Nadal—by this point no longer looking like a dignified European in a smart pinstripe suit, but rather like a man who'd just gotten off a red-eye—stood with his fist pumped. 7–7.

The tournament supervisors had made the decision that only two more games could be played before the match would have to be postponed on account of darkness. Though this wasn't conveyed to the players, intuitively they both sensed it. In the photographers' pit behind the court, dozens of shooters changed lenses and attached devices to their cameras to compensate for the fading light.

Regardless of the progressing dusk, Nadal picked up Federer's serves, returning every offering deep in the court. After winning two of the first three points, Nadal was obliged to hit a backhand a good two yards behind the baseline. Using his dominant right hand to guide the ball, he muscled a crosscourt winner, a shot most players wouldn't have had the audacity to attempt, much less stick. In the NBC commentary booth behind the baseline, McEnroe stood up and mimicked the shot as he spoke.

Unbowed, Federer squeezed off his twenty-fifth ace and then won a point when Nadal slipped on a wet patch of grass. Federer saved still another break point with a masterful serve to the corner. And then, inexplicably, he lapsed. On an inside-out forehand—the very stroke he had executed so well for the past three sets—Federer went for a winner straight up the line, over the high point of the net. It was another example of Nadal's pressure causing an opponent to go for broke. Federer mistimed the bounce and batted the ball into the net.

On Nadal's fourth break point of the game, Federer positioned himself to hit a forehand that bounced near the T of the service line, in the dead center of the court. This may be the single most elemental shot in tennis, the stroke and distance

most teaching pros use when instructing beginners. Splaying
his legs and taking a bigger cut at the ball than the situation
dictated, Federer smacked the shot a few inches beyond the
baseline. He appeared to have blurted out "*Nie,*" the German
word for "never," as the ball sailed long. In Nadal's box, his entourage formed a group hug. Except for Uncle Toni, who retreated alone to the aisle, too nervous for human interaction.
8–7.

Head down, Federer walked disconsolately to his chair. He
sipped from his Evian bottle and tossed it over his shoulder
in frustration, but not before first screwing on the cap. (Even
his mini-tantrums are considerate in their way.) Nadal swigged
from his Evian bottle, trying "not to think about anything too
much." Straining to be heard over the crowd's roar, Maria an-
nounced the score and added a pertinent piece of information
before the game began. "New balls, please."

There was one game left—victory or darkness—and Nadal would have the advantage of playing with fresh balls. He
popped out of his chair like a jack-in-the-box and jogged to
the baseline before serving for the Wimbledon title. On the
first point, the new ball trampolined off the polyester strings
of Nadal's racket and his nervous forehand sailed long. In this,
the sixty-second game of the match, it was just his twenty-sev-
enth unforced error.

Nadal then made an eloquent statement about both his res-
ervoir of courage and his underrated tactical savvy. For the first
time in the entire match he serve-and-volleyed. After spinning
a serve (where else?) deep to Federer's backhand, Nadal followed his forward momentum. Federer's return wafted in the
air, presenting Nadal with the simplest forehand volley. It was
the perfect strategy at the perfect time. This wasn't just a testament to Nadal's guts; it was a testament to his tennis cortex

too, a sharp rejoinder to the critics who dismiss him as brutal and machine-like. He had lost the previous point from the baseline, so he figured he'd try something new.

15–15. As if awakened to the virtues of net play, Nadal won the next point at the net as well, driving Federer off the court and punching away another forehand volley. 30–15. Nadal approached the net again. This third time, Federer ripped a passing shot that Nadal could only stab into the air and beyond the baseline. Still, two out of three ain't bad. 30–30.

As if the match needed more complications, a light began to flicker behind the court: a malfunctioning panel on the bottom of the scoreboard, as it turned out. Already annoyed by all the ambient imperfection—the rain delays, the diminishing light, the boisterous crowd—Federer shook his head in frustration and pointed out the distracting light to Pascal Maria. The umpire appeared confused but, recognizing that this was not the time for protracted discourse, leaned into the microphone. "Please don't use cameras with flashes."

Nadal played conservatively and coaxed a backhand error from Federer. It was 40–30, championship point. Toni Nadal rose from his seat and stood in the aisle next to his brother Sebastian. Behind the baseline Bjorn Borg sat erect. Diane Morales, well-adjusted Memphis high school Spanish teacher turned Nadal sorceress, yelled to her daughter. Still convinced that her viewing would bring Nadal bad luck, she'd been surreptitiously checking the live scores on-line. "It's Rafa!" she shrieked, loud enough to be heard in eastern Arkansas, as she scrambled to turn on the TV. "He's at match point!"

The court may have appeared reasonably well lit on television, but this was a distortion; in reality, it might as well have been illuminated with toy flashlights. Yet when Nadal, on his third championship point, spun another serve to his backhand, Federer, as if wearing night-vision goggles, saw the ball perfectly. He turned and flicked a delicate, sharply angled backhand crosscourt for a winner. In retrospect, there was something terribly poignant about this shot. It wasn't a cold-cocked, nothing-to-lose blast. It was less a hit than a massage. It was one last flourish, one last dash of artistry, one last display of Soft Power, before the mighty king was deposed.

If Federer had just shown off his gift for shotmaking, Nadal then displayed his gift of fearlessness. Unbothered by losing his *third* match point, he maintained his ritual and released a 115 mph serve. Federer logically guessed backhand. But Nadal won still another tactical battle, painting the forehand corner of the box, out of reach. Championship point number four.

Blocking out the chorus of "Come on, Rafa," Nadal wiped his face, bounced the ball seven times, and hit a cautious first serve followed by a cautious backhand. The ball landed barely behind the service line but took a tricky bounce, darting to the right. Nothing drastic, but it was enough to throw off Federer's timing. And it was a reminder that for all the virtues that make up a seminal sporting event, there is also a component of luck.

Federer swung forcefully but awkwardly, his arms moving forward while his body weight jerked laterally. As ever, he stared at the ball as it left his strings. The shot was impeded by the top of the net and died on his own side of the court. 9–7.

The ball hadn't come to a full rest when Nadal dropped to the grass and fell flat on his back as if he had been shot. He had Wimbledon. The fans rose as one, cheering hysterically at the final scene of a drama that had lasted four hours and forty-eight minutes. Television commentators stayed silent, letting the images speak for themselves. The Nadal contingent hugged. The message board traffic exploded.

One final touch from the chair umpire, Pascal Maria. As Nadal rolled on the ground, breading himself in grass, Maria said firmly, "Game, set, and match. Rafael Nadal. Six-four, six-four, six-seven, six-seven, nine-seven." It was superfluous, and it was pitch-perfect.

It was 9:16 at night when the scoreboard finally froze.

Those with a thing for symbolism might have noticed that the Rolex logo above Federer's name on the scoreboard featured a crown adorned with five — not six — points. Bjorn Borg's record of five straight Wimbledon titles wouldn't be eclipsed; his distinction of being the last man to have won the French Open and Wimbledon in the same summer, well, that no longer held. Now it was Nadal. In 2007, it was Federer who had stopped Nadal's record clay court winning streak at eighty-one matches. Now Nadal had broken Federer's record of sixty-five straight grass court wins.

Two punch-drunk fighters, Federer and Nadal met at the net, exchanged a power-clasp handshake, and walked off the court with their arms wrapped around each other's waist. After seven hours of the most intimate relations, they at last made physical contact. As they shuffled to their chairs, Nadal gave Federer one last slap on the back. Not for nothing do they call this a gentleman's game.

Nadal whipped off his headband, literally letting his hair down for the first time all day. Arms raised in the air — applauding the crowd whose emotional investment had so handsomely paid off — Nadal made what's become a ritual leap onto the roof of the NBC commentary booth and into the box where his knot of supporters was waiting. Nadal hugged his group and his uncle Toni, his sweaty head buried in chests and shoulders. Recognizing the national significance — *patria!* — Nadal carried a Spanish flag and made his way to the Royal Box, where Crown Prince Felipe and Princess Letizia had been seated.

All the while, Robert Federer looked on, smiling and smacking his meaty hands together in applause. Behind him, Lynette was standing and applauding too. Sure, they'd wished like hell that their son had been the winner. And they were somewhat concerned with how Roger would handle this defeat. But what a sporting event! "Hell of a match, hell of a catfight," Robert Federer said in uncomplaining summary. And his disappointment was tempered by feelings of genuine happiness for the Nadal clan. "They're such a nice family and we'd always had a good relationship with them, and now they could experience having their boy win Wimbledon," he said. "Honestly, a few days later, there was this pressure, I don't know how else to describe it"—here, he points to his thick chest—"and it didn't feel nice. Not at all. But right after the match? No, I didn't suffer."

Both players took turns holding their trophies aloft. Dusk having morphed into full-on darkness, Federer and Nadal were backlit only by the popping flashbulbs. White-clad figures amid the blackness, they looked like a pair of ghosts. The thunderous applause continued. In the unfamiliar position of Wimbledon runner-up, Federer was interviewed on the court. He cobbled together the following: "Yeah, I tried everything. It got a little late and everything. But, look, Rafa's a deserving champion. He just played fantastically . . . Yeah, [the darkness] didn't make it easier, but you got to expect the worst. And it's the worst opponent on the best court. No, but it's been a joy again to play here. A pity I couldn't win it under the circumstances, but I'll be back next year."

Fittingly, Nadal matched Federer grace note for grace note. Did beating Federer in such an epic make the occasion more special? "Well, for sure, you know, win Roger here after five years, I lost the last two finals, close finals. But he's still the number one. He's still the best. He's still five-time champion here. Right now I have one, so for me it's very, very important day."

Nadal posed with the trophy, the Challenge Cup, and bit the handle, another Nadal infantilizing ritual, this one tracing to the first time he won a tournament as a kid. The players orbited the perimeter of the court in opposite directions, each carrying his award. Spontaneously, they slapped five as they passed.

Meanwhile, John McEnroe had shuffled out of the NBC booth and positioned himself between the lip of the court and the clubhouse. At Grand Slam events, the winning and losing finalists are, ahem, strongly encouraged to conduct a post-match interview with the largest television rights holder, in this case NBC. While Federer surely would rather have forfeited his £375,000 check than rehash his stinging defeat just minutes after the match had ended, he was intercepted by McEnroe. Federer being Federer, he relented.

Having spent the preceding seven hours, including rain delays, calling the match, McEnroe was emotionally exhausted himself. McEnroe closed the distance on Federer and started not with a question but with a proclamation. "Listen, Roger, first of all can I just say thank you, as a tennis player, that you allowed us to be part of this amazing spectacle."

A producer in McEnroe's ear told him, in so many words, to stop the monologue and ask a question.

McEnroe obliged. "Is that any consolation?"

"A little bit," mumbled Federer, backing away subtly. "Thanks, John. It's tough, it's tough. It hurts," he said, raising his fingers to his already glistening eyes, the levees about to be breached.

At that point, Nadal walked into the back of the frame, gripping the trophy. He had the good sense to stop in his tracks.

In the background, the crowd's cheer of "Rafa! Rafa!" was still audible. McEnroe continued. "It was the greatest match that I ever witnessed. So much drama, I mean you must have thought that after all that you'd gone through in that fourth set you were gonna get that done at the end."

His voice catching, Federer grimaced. "I was hoping to, yeah, I had that break point, but Rafa"—even in stinging defeat, he referred to Nadal by his affectionate nickname—"really served so well throughout the match, he didn't give me too many chances even though I won sets three and four. I missed so many opportunities maybe in the first two sets and maybe I paid a price in the end. But, uh, Rafa did well."

Now Federer's face looked as if it were caving in on itself. Endorphins were still racing through his system, but he was coming down off his adrenaline high. McEnroe continued. "It's got to be, listen, I know you're feeling so much emotion right now." As every junior high school guidance counselor knows, you don't broach the topic of emotion to someone on the verge of tears. At the very mention of the word "emotion," Federer recoiled. Sensing that Federer was incapable of saying anything else, McEnroe placed his hand on Federer's left shoulder. "I want to . . . come here. Gimme a hug because, thank you, man. Thank you, thank you so much, okay?" As Federer nodded and walked away, McEnroe needed a second to swallow and collect himself. And if you ever doubted the transformative impact of a tennis match, well, here it was. McEnroe, tennis's erstwhile bad boy, had suddenly reinvented himself as Oprah.

Federer walked hurriedly to the locker room with his head low, like a man caught without an umbrella trying to avoid the rain. He plopped down on the bench. His tears mingled with his sweat, but he was too depleted, physically and emotionally, for the heaving, keening sobs he was otherwise capable of unleashing. A friend who visited the locker room characterized Federer as looking "totally devastated, almost like he was in a state of shock." His phone was filling up with text messages. "Bad luck, too bad there had to be a loser in that one," read one. It encouraged him to take pride in the way he and Nadal had lifted the sport beyond the usual audience. The sender was Pete Sampras.

Like mourners attending a wake, supporters filed into the locker room to offer their condolences. Sometimes Federer looked up, his eyes rimmed in red. Other times not. Outside the locker room, it fell to Robert Federer to gently inform various Swiss dignitaries that Roger wasn't up to receiving guests at the moment, no matter how well intentioned they were.

This was unquestionably the low point of Federer's career. Losing to Nadal, that was nothing new. But losing to Nadal at Wimbledon, the tournament he had not merely won, but *ruled* every year since 2003? That was something else entirely. Something deeper, more crucial. That Nadal would now almost assuredly inherit Federer's top ranking seemed to make official the transfer of power. This was defeat distilled to its essence. This was the seemingly insurmountable Man o' War losing to the horse Upset, an event so momentous it would spawn a new phrase in the sports lexicon. This was the great John L. Sullivan losing to Gentleman Jim Corbett, Y. A. Tittle kneeling in the mud of the football field, blood streaming down his face.

Afflicted with a kind of survivor's guilt — just as he'd been four Sundays before in Paris — Nadal let Federer have the locker room to himself. Nadal went to his anti-doping test and hugged family members in the corridors. When well-wishers attempted to deliver celebratory champagne they were turned away. Even at this moment, the apex of his career, Nadal was mindful that bringing his giddy entourage into the locker room would have added to Federer's despair.

Over the years, Federer had developed a ritual. In the hours after winning a Major title, he would spark up his computer, read the glowing accounts, see the triumphant photos, and watch the highlights on YouTube. "I like seeing what the fans saw and experienced," he says. "You miss that playing." On this night, he would have no use for his computer, no interest in watching clips of Nadal holding up the trophy. ("It's something I don't ever want to see," Federer said two months later.) Back at his rental house, he had a quiet dinner of take-out pizza with his entourage, played some cards in silence, and fell asleep. He booked a short vacation to Corsica the next day, and he couldn't get on that plane fast enough.

He would experience an unfortunate truism of tennis: 128 players will enter a Major tournament, and 127 will start the next event on a losing streak. And he would experience this irony: for years he did virtually nothing wrong. Yet all those casual fans were going to know him as the loser of the Greatest Match Ever. A few days later, Federer made the cover of *Sports Illustrated* for the first time. He was gaining more renown in defeat than he had for any of his triumphs.

It was almost unendurably sad seeing a champion so thoroughly damaged. But Federer had shown plenty in defeat. He had scraped and fought and revealed himself to be so much more than merely a gifted artist. The suggestion that he would emulate Borg and vanish, too precious to indulge the rivalry and/or his own mortality? That was extinguished two months later when Federer—though seeded second for the first time in four years—would salvage his season by winning the 2008 U.S. Open, the very next Major on the calendar, beating Andy Murray in the final. No post-traumatic stress here. The assault on Mount Sampras was rejoined; history was back on notice.* In a perverse way, though, this loss in the Greatest Match Ever Played, and his recovery, ultimately did as much to burnish Federer's image as if he had won Wimbledon outright. Here was the personification of those lines from Kipling emblazoned above Centre Court. The real hallmark of a man is his ability to handle defeat as well as victory.

Deliriously happy, the vamosbrigade brigade continued their texting and message board posting into the night. In Austin, Texas, Andy Roddick finally walked out of the airport, marveling over his colleagues' performance. In the United Kingdom at 9:20 P.M., there was a 1,400-megawatt spike in electricity, the equivalent of more than half a million teakettles boiling at once. A spokeswoman for the British National Grid told reporters that the surge was caused by Wimbledon viewers who'd been so transfixed that they couldn't leave the sofa to switch on the lights until after the match had ended.

In the French hamlet of Naves, Peter Carry and his weekend guests, having canceled their dinner reservations to watch the conclusion of the match, drove into a neighboring town for pizza. They arrived to find the proprietor turning away customers. Though hardly complaining, the man explained that everyone in town had been captivated by the match, delayed their dinner plans, and come to his pizzeria for late sustenance. He had exhausted his supply of dough.

At the All England Club, the fans who had bonded over the communal experience finally filed out of the gates. A crew disengaged the nets and ripped up the swatches of worn ryegrass. The stadium that had been suffused with so much cheering

---

* At least until Federer fell in five sets to Nadal in the 2009 Australian Open final, one more installment in the rivalry.

now echoed with the clang of temporary structures being dis-assembled and the crackle of security radios. On the wim bledon.org website, an alert staffer toggled a key and started up the Countdown to Wimbledon 2009. Only 350 days, 15 hours, 27 minutes, and 44 seconds to go.

Still high on adrenaline, Pascal Maria walked off the court and went looking for his wife. As the chair umpire for the final match, he was invited to attend the Champions Ball (much) later in the evening. He planned to go back to his rental house, take a shower, and change into formalwear. But his mind raced as he replayed points and reconstructed dialogue. He was duty-bound to maintain an arm's-length relationship with all the players, but he felt intense emotion for Federer and Nadal. "They are the crème," he said, "true champions, both of them. They're not just tennis winners but real champions."

He held his wife's hand as they walked through the cata-combs of the stadium and off the grounds. They joked that she had picked a hell of a first match to attend. "You don't need to watch tennis again," he told her. "It's just going to dis-appoint you." He had been on the court for seven exhilarat-ing hours, and while he hadn't been the focus of the match, he'd been plenty prominent. Yet he went unrecognized. He walked past hundreds of fans who'd been transfixed by the match and none broke stride as they walked by him. To the third man on the court for the Greatest Tennis Match Ever Played, that was the highest compliment he could possibly have been paid.

Federer's devoted army of supporters cast this loss to Nadal as outright tragedy. Evil had defeated good, violence beaten peace, darkness trumped light. A friend of mine who had watched the match from Centre Court's row M likened the result to "watching an angel fall." No, wait, it was "the col-lapse of a belief system." Reflecting on the match two months

later, even Federer remarked, "I think more people left feeling
sorry for me than they were happy for Rafa, which hurts me
a little."* But really, that missed the point. It was impossible
not to see truth and light and artistry — albeit in a different
form — in Nadal's performance.

When Nadal made his way to the interview room he was
nearly helpless to articulate his feelings. "Impossible to describe, no? I don't know. Just very happy. Is unbelievable for
me have a title here in Wimbledon. Is probably — well, is a
dream. I always, when I was a kid, I dream for play here, but
for win is amazing, no?" Perhaps this was just a function of
trying to describe the indescribable in a nonnative tongue. But
his remarks to the Spanish media were similar. "It feels like
a dream. My first Wimbledon? Beating Federer, the greatest
player of all time? A match like this? How could it *not* feel like
a dream?"

As Nadal walked around the complex, the knee he had
tweaked in the third set — it seemed like days ago — began
throbbing. Though Nadal's house was barely a hundred meters
from the All England Club, he sheepishly asked for a courtesy
car to transport him the short distance. Television and print
reporters and cameramen from networks that were not Wimbledon rights holders, and thus not allowed to broadcast on
the grounds, had staked out Nadal's house. When he arrived,
Nadal stood at his front door to accommodate the interview
requests.

Afterward, as the car waited, Nadal changed into a tuxedo

---

* In fairness, perhaps sensing the awkwardness, Federer quickly added, "At
the same time, I appreciate that tennis went up a notch with that match, and
that's what I strove to do in my five years as number one, to make tennis better, more popular, and I admit that that Wimbledon final achieved all I had
wanted, even if I lost it."

and headed to the Champions Ball. It was past midnight when he walked in. The crowd of five hundred bestowed on Nadal one last standing ovation of the day. Oddly enough, Venus Williams, who had been waiting for hours, arrived a few moments later. "That was an incredible match," she said. "Yours too," he responded. As Nadal worked the room, shaking hands and posing for photos, his parents and grandparents ate dessert, the only course still being served.

It was close to 4 A.M. when he got back to the house. He took one last massage from Maymo, as his Nike representative and his publicist sat alongside the table. In another era, the Wimbledon champion might have spent the night in an alcohol-fueled celebration. In a truly postmodern moment, while Nadal got his rubdown, friends toggled with their BlackBerrys and phones, reading aloud from the hundreds of congratulatory text messages and e-mails they'd already received.

In a few hours, a car would take Nadal to the airport. He would make a brief stop in Germany, where he would apologize in person for withdrawing from the Stuttgart tournament. He'd stop in Barcelona and see a doctor who would examine his knee. By late afternoon, Nadal would be back in Majorca, greeted like a conquering hero. Within a month, it would be official: after 160 weeks—more than three years!—he earned his promotion from number two. And to complete his gilded summer, he would win the singles gold medal at the Beijing Olympics.

Now, though, Nadal lay in bed, and for the first time all day he would be alone with his thoughts, trying to make some sense of the past twenty-four hours. He had finally won Wimbledon, his career ambition, and had done so in front of his family and friends and royalty from his country. He had prevailed in a competition that would reset the standard for tennis excellence. It was made all the more meaningful by his opponent, his rival, his conjoined colleague, the player who pushed him and tested him like no one else on the planet. As Nadal replayed the day, splicing a personal highlight reel in his head, he felt the sweetness of having surpassed his own expectations.

Wimbledon 2008

GENTLEMEN'S SINGLES
FINAL STATISTICS

Federer	4	4	7^7	7^{10}	7
Nadal	6	6	6^5	6^8	9

	FEDERER (Switzerland)	NADAL (Spain)
1st serve %	128 of 195 = 66%	159 of 218 = 73%
Aces	25	6
Double faults	2	3
Unforced errors	52	27
Winning % on 1st serve	93 of 128 = 73%	110 of 159 = 69%
Winning % on 2nd serve	38 of 67 = 57%	35 of 59 = 59%
Receiving points won	73 of 218 = 33%	64 of 195 = 33%
Break point conversions	1 of 13 = 8%	4 of 13 = 31%
Net approaches	42 of 75 = 56%	22 of 31 = 71%
Total points won	204	209
Fastest serve	129 mph	120 mph
Average 1st serve speed	117 mph	112 mph
Average 2nd serve speed	100 mph	93 mph

Compiled by Wimbledon Information System / IBM

Acknowledgments

Much the way that tennis players might aspire to the heights of Federer or Nadal—unattainable as that ideal might be—as I wrote this book, John McPhee's *Levels of the Game* was never far from my thoughts. A classic by any definition, *Levels* masterfully braids various themes and ruminations and personality profiles around a 1968 U.S. Open match between Arthur Ashe and Clark Graebner.

McPhee is a Hall of Fame writer. In this case, he also had the good fortune of covering athletes at a time when they were far more accessible than they are today. McPhee reportedly procured from CBS three reels of tape, rented a movie projector, and met the subjects in a hotel room in the Caribbean. Over the course of several days, they reconstructed the match, point by point. Suffice to say, forty years later, I was not afforded the chance to replicate this drill with Federer, Nadal, and a DVD of the 2008 Wimbledon final. I have, however, been fortunate over the years to have spent a good deal of time with both athletes, usually in the course of my tennis coverage for *Sports Illustrated,* and many of the players' quotes in this book are derived from those interviews as well as from press conferences.

While neither player affirmatively attached his name to this project—or, for that matter, received compensation—neither did they do anything to impede my work. A good thing this, as I relied on many others for background information, anecdotes, and technical expertise.

The tennis circuit is often characterized as a "traveling road show." But it also takes on the dimensions of a close-knit community. There's plenty of internecine fighting, and there are rivalries that play out with far less dignity and positive outcomes than Federer-Nadal. But there's also respect and support and a prevailing sense that in the end we're united, not least by a common fondness for this mesmerizing sport.

In the course of this project, I witnessed the best of Tennis Nation, and everyone from Pete Sampras and Martina Navratilova to volunteer ushers assisted me in some way, shape, or form. I relied on too many people to catalog them here, but I owe special thanks to Graeme Agars, Nicola Arzani, Antoine Ballon, Madeleine Bärlocher, Per Bastholt, Philippe Bouin, Peter Carry, Chris Clarey, Sarah Clarke, Bud Collins, Nolo Colonia, Jim Courier, Martin Cruddace, Tim Curry, Sally Duncan, Brad Faulkner, Robert Federer, Steve Flink, Andrew Friedman, Justin Gimelstob, Sven Groeneveld, Martin Guntrip, Eben Harrell, Paul Hawkins, Pete Holtermann, David Law, Andrew Lawrence, Jon Levey, Pascal Maria, Stuart Miller, Diane Morales, Toni Nadal, Dave Nagle, Linda Pearce, Benito Perez-Barbadillo, Eleanor Preston, Roman Prokes, Ted Robinson, Perry Rogers, Greg Sharko, Miki Singh, René Stauffer, Kate Tuckwell, Mats Wilander, John Yandell, Neus Yerro, and assorted deep throats—you know who you are.

Jeff Spielberger, Tom Tebbutt, Tom Perrotta, and Chris Hunt read and critiqued various drafts of the manuscript, improving it immeasurably. Pete Bodo was instrumental from the beginning in helping me flesh out the ideas for the book. My agent, Scott Waxman, and editor, Susan Canavan, were diligent as ever in making this project a reality. Larry Cooper proved, again, that he is the Federer-Nadal of copyediting. Thanks, too, to the si.com Tennis Mailbag Readers for their observations, encouragement, kind words, dissenting opinions, and (gulp) ten years of weekly fun.

As always, my final thanks to Allegra, Ben, and Ellie, who provided support and love and relative quiet while I spent three crazy months engrossed in tennis. At least it wasn't cage fighting.

LJW
February 11, 2009